THE
THEATRE
OF
COMMITMENT

Eric Bentley

THE
THEATRE
OF
COMMITMENT

*AND OTHER ESSAYS
ON DRAMA IN OUR SOCIETY*

METHUEN & CO LTD
11 New Fetter Lane London E.C.4

FOR PETER

"Was mich nicht umbringt, macht mich stärker."

. . . . we live in a period of social passions. The tragedy of our period lies in the conflict between the individual and the collectivity, or in the conflict between two hostile collectivities in the same individual.

LEON TROTSKY
Literature and Revolution

CONTENTS

PREFACE   xi

IS THE DRAMA AN EXTINCT SPECIES?   3

THE AMERICAN DRAMA, 1944–1954   18

WHAT IS THEATRE?   47

TAKING IBSEN PERSONALLY   98

THE PRO AND CON OF POLITICAL THEATRE   119

LETTER TO A WOULD-BE PLAYWRIGHT   160

THE THEATRE OF COMMITMENT   190

NOTES AND ACKNOWLEDGMENTS   232

INDEX   235

PREFACE

IN *The New Masses* of February 27, 1945, there
was a review of my first book which the reviewer
himself described as "largely negative." However,
he also said I had dealt "with profound questions
which few critics of our times have touched," and
it is of interest—to me, at least—to note which of
these questions he regarded as "the key moral
question" even though it is one he said I raised
but failed to deal with:

> It seems to me that Mr. Bentley is fighting, in
> the pages of his own book, . . . an uncon-
> cluded battle of his own. He is tormented by
> what he conceives as the conflicting claims of
> the individual and the collective.

Now this was very true, even though that book
had begun as an academic exercise; and I am
afraid that, as I write these words twenty-two years
later, the battle remains unconcluded.

The seven essays in the present volume, having
been written over a period of a dozen years or so,
do not show their author in one consistent stance,

and the inconsistency is precisely the one which *The New Masses'* analysis would lead the reader to expect. Though the thinking might claim to be consistently liberal, the liberalism tends sometimes toward the individualistic, sometimes toward the collectivistic pole. It might be hard to answer such a question as: is the author pro-Communist?

Still, there is, I believe, another constant in my viewpoint besides liberalism: I am a socialist and have been for thirty years. If my attitude to the Communist Party has varied, that, surely, need not be viewed as purely *my* problem. The Communist Party has varied and is varying. Not being a member of it, nor otherwise awestruck, I propose to judge each of its policies on its merits. I shall be anti-Communist if that means I shall on occasion oppose measures which this Communist Party or that advocates; I shall not be anti-Communist if that is to imply that all decisions of all Communist Parties are bound to be wrong or that "Communism" is a good name for all that is bad and is therefore the opposite of a "freedom" which embodies all that is good.

It is curious to see McGeorge Bundy go before the television cameras armed with quotations provided by his research assistants showing that Hans Morgenthau, down the years, has made some political predictions which didn't come true. Couldn't that be done to any political commentator except a very wary and evasive one? In any case, Mr. Morgenthau was not asking to be accepted as a prophet. He was not asking for personal acceptance at all. It is a matter of indifference what his readers think of *him*. He offers facts and arguments which are either cogent in their own right or are not: he is not asking that they be accepted on *his* authority but on theirs. The same applies to Walter Lippmann. What he says now about Vietnam cannot be discredited by citation of opinions in his past that may not commend themselves to us. We should not be concerned with *his* personal record but with the issues he is calling our attention to.

With such matters in mind, I have not been concerned to touch up my own personal record. It is not that I pride myself on contradicting myself, as Walt Whitman did—he had genius as his excuse, and in any case was writing poetry, not criticism—but that, in trying to give a better impression of myself, I would be simplifying what is more important here: my subject. If, for example, I were to try to bring the earlier essays here printed into line with the later, I would only succeed in suggesting that the later lay claim to finality. Yet they too, if personally considered, represent but stages along life's way, and if, as I am asking, they be considered *im*personally, they should benefit by interaction, in the reader's mind, with the earlier pieces. For if the whole truth transcends the whole of this book, the whole of this book, I confidently assume, transcends any part of it, even those parts closest to my heart at the present moment.

Our culture, especially the academic part of it, values timelessness, and tends to respect a critic for whatever gift he may have for getting outside the moment at which he writes. Thus, the very failure to respond to the moment at which one writes comes to be regarded as a positive merit—impotent men can always be complimented on their chastity. Surely there are good, as well as bad, responses to the moment, and we should welcome writers whose responses to the moment we consider serviceable: Heaven knows there are not many of them.

Timelessness not being among the objectives of the essays collected here, I can say of the attendant risks that I took them with my eyes open. Better to err with Lippmann and Morgenthau than to play it safe with Mr. X and Professor Y. What respect is due to a book that praises commitment but makes none?

E. B.

SPRING *1967*

THE
THEATRE
OF
COMMITMENT

IS THE DRAMA AN EXTINCT SPECIES?

NOBODY DISPUTES that something is wrong. People have been saying that it's because the theatre is badly organized, and other people have been replying: not at all, it's simply that there's a dearth of good plays. There being a good deal of truth on both sides, it may be wise to sort out some of the points.

To begin with "good plays." One is concerned with two orders of merit not always clearly enough distinguished: talent and genius. Genius lies to a great extent outside any useful discussion because nothing we can say or do will produce it. It comes uncalled for or not at all. What can be discussed is the welcome we give it. And the sad fact is that we welcome it too little and too late. We welcome it when it is safe to do so, when it is practically impossible not to do so. The great modern example is Bernard Shaw. To have welcomed him in

B

3

the Eighteen Nineties, when he was "dangerous," would have been enterprising. To accept him after 1910, as the theatre mostly did, was to accept the accepted. By that time the public had learned how to ward off Shaw's blows: critics thought him a clown, admirers thought him a classic; whichever way you look at it, he was through.

Since the death of Shaw, how many geniuses are left in the field? Readers will agree that they are few, even if they don't accept my nominations. And among the few I should have liked to nominate some are not accurately defined as playwrights. Charlie Chaplin and Eduardo De Filippo, though they have taken on the dramatist's tasks and performed them admirably, achieve greatness in the composite capacity of actor-playwright, a special and perhaps indissoluble union of actor, role and author. I am left, it seems to me, with but two names: Bertolt Brecht and Sean O'Casey. Yet even two are enough to make us modify the proposition that there are no new plays for us to do. The plays are there. The question is why we don't do them. The answer cannot lie wholly in their authors' politics which are (for present purposes) not very different from Shaw's. It lies, rather, in Time: Brecht and O'Casey are now where Shaw was before 1910. When they have "dated," Broadway will announce that they are "timely."

4

Genius, notoriously, is tardily recognized in all the arts. One cannot be surprised at this. One's surprise should rather be reserved for the fact that there is genius in the offing at all. If economic history goes slump-boom, slump-boom, the history of playwriting, one is tempted to say, goes slump-slump-slump. The dramatic critic is not called upon to explain why at any given moment there are no great playrights. Empirical reasoning would more probably lead him to argue that there never could be a great playwright, just as empirical reasoning would lead a moralist to argue that there could never be a saint. You are not surprised to find money changers in the temple; the surprising sight is Christ with a whip. One is amazed at Shakespeare and Ibsen; Thomas Dekker and Henry Arthur Jones one takes for granted.

However—or rather, consequently—it is much more with the Dekkers and Joneses that we must be concerned. They, if anyone, are our regular stand-bys; their presence is not just an occasional blessing, it is something we require; it belongs to the minimum demands of theatre. In a world of two billion inhabitants it is fair to assume that there are always thousands of them. This means that if we can justly complain of a dearth of plays we are not so much protesting that very little genius exists as implying that talent, though it

5

exists, is being deflected into other channels. The Dekkers and Joneses exist but are not writing plays.

So much the better for them. It is all too likely that the artistic impulse—the dramatic impulse particularly—can best find satisfaction today outside the arts altogether. There is the drama of science; and even the drama of politics need not be contemptible. Among our young people I find the artistic temperament, characterized by moral sensibility and vital energy, in undergraduates who will be chemists, lawyers and doctors, more than in graduate students who will be professionally occupied with the arts. Those in whom the need for literary expression is irrepressible write fiction or poetry, in either of which modes they can work unbullied by boobs, and in one of which they might even make a living. (Sometimes I think all our poetic and fictional talent today is dramatic talent scared away by the idiocy of the theatre. Certainly, if Ernest Hemingway or Robert Penn Warren could devote ten years to theatrical work he would write even the best of our playwrights off the stage.)

Nor can anyone pretend that TV and the movies attract only the less gifted. The time has gone by, if it ever existed, when the average film is inferior to the average play. Indeed, certain stage forms have been superseded and rendered obsolete by the movies. Once *A Prisoner of Zenda* has been on the screen, you would never want to see it on the stage. Pictures like *The Treasure of Sierra Madre* and *High Noon* transcend all the theatre's efforts to present adventure. I can explain the drama critics' enthusiasm for the current thriller *Dial M for Murder* only on the assumption that they don't go to the movies.

In short, playwriting talent has been deflected along with the theatre public into TV, the movies, poetry, the novel or out of the arts altogether, with the result that (to coin a phrase) "there is no American drama." There is a lack not only of Shakespeares and O'Caseys but also of Dekkers and Joneses. In America playwriting is not yet a profession.

Playwriting may be said to be a profession when playwrights of high average talent are given their chance, their chance being production by performers who also constitute a profession. The American theatre does not offer playwrights this chance. A play cannot be produced on Broadway unless its producers think it is likely to run for a year. Plays of "mere promise" are excluded; the theatre is a place where promises are not kept. Hence, though there is a place for the playwright to "succeed," there is no place for him to begin or to develop.

7

It has been said: "Without *Titus Andronicus,* no *Hamlet.*" Yet if a Shakespeare came along today, what would happen? Either *Titus* would never get produced at all; or it would be a flop and drive the Bard to drink, teaching, and TV; or it would be a hit, and the poet would spend an anxious lifetime writing twenty more *Tituses.*

A profession of playwrights, I have intimated, presupposes a profession of actors. Despite Actors' Equity Association, there is no such profession, there are merely some arrangements to stop employers' running off with their workers' wages. An adequate definition of an acting profession would include what the French understand by métier—a standard of workmanship that you achieve by joining the group and by practice; as with playwrights, the lack is apprenticeship in the beginning and continuity later. You do not know what the art of acting is capable of unless you have seen an ensemble of players who have worked together, year in, year out.

In the matter of acting, America has much to learn from some other countries—notably, France, Germany, and Russia. (I don't know enough about the Orient to justify any Eastern representation.) In the matter of playwriting, I know of but one country where things are, perhaps, in a healthier state than here, and that is France. Only in

Paris, it seems to me, have we today * the impression that playwriting is a profession. A literate play stands the same chance of professional performance that, with us, a novel stands of publication. There is consequently a large band of playwrights who in Paris are regular and commercial and over here are (or would be) *avant garde:* for example, Achard, Anouilh, Obey, Salacrou. There is also an overlap with poetry and the novel, as the names of Cocteau, Mauriac, Montherlant and Sartre testify. Even the most "unplayable" poet is played: I saw *Le Soulier de Satin* and *Partage de Midi* lavishly staged in two of the largest theatres.

In England an "unpopular" poet like M. Claudel might well be broadcast on the Third Programme; he'd never reach the West End stage unless he were willing, like Mr. Eliot in *The Cocktail Party*, to reach it on its own terms. Shakespeare continues to use up the best energies of English theatre. London produces him and ignores Mr. O'Casey today, exactly as it produced him and ignored Shaw in the Nineties. Italy, ever as poor in drama as she is rich in theatricality, is finding that a profession of playwrights cannot be legislated into existence even with the help of subsidies. Ger-

* 1953–54. In the Sixties, Germany was to take the lead. See p. 200 ff. below. *This note, like all the others marked with an asterisk, was added in 1967; the numbered footnotes belong to the time of writing.*

many is the living proof that a well-organized and decentralized repertory system does not necessarily, or at any rate immediately, produce its own dramatists. It is amazing to think for how little time the German theatres were not playing. Goebbels closed them when he proclaimed total mobilization in 1944. By 1945 most of them were destroyed by bombs anyway. But the actors were at work again as soon as the war ended. Since then the old buildings have been repaired or new ones built. That there are no new playwrights only proves that there is a deeper damage than that of air-raids. Somewhere a nerve had been cut.

Soviet Russia I do not know at firsthand. Russian movies suggest directly, reports of reliable witnesses suggest indirectly, that the Russians still have the greatest profession of actors in the world. What one knows of their playwrights is less pleasant. If the degree of organization were the criterion, I imagine the Russian playwrights are the most "professional" in the world. But if the criterion is organization at all, it is organization to a certain end, namely, enabling playwrights to grow to their full stature. Russia offsets the gift of a fabulous theatre and a good living with a heavy price in censorial restrictions. To the observation that Shakespeare also worked under a censorship, I can only reply that it is open to anyone to compare

Elizabethan with Soviet censorship, both as to the regulations and their enforcement. In such a comparison, the Queen, and even the Puritan city fathers with whom she had little in common, will make a good showing. If some of the Puritans would have been as strict as Stalin, had they had the opportunity, it remains important that they did not have the opportunity.

A comparison of the two epochs and regimes could not be made at all except that we still tend to think of censorship in an old-fashioned way. We think of particular acts of censorship, the striking out of a forbidden word, the banning of a single book. We have barely realized that a greater efficiency in censorship has brought in its train a new mentality both in the censors and their victims. I have in mind not only the more macabre horrors of the situation but also the prosaic dullness of Soviet intellectuals. It resembles all too closely the dullness of the bourgeoisie against which all left-wing movements, as far as the intelligentsia is concerned, were a revolt.

Not long ago, two American playwrights said in *The New York Times* that the American drama was threatened by the totalitarian mentality—in this case represented by the anti-red Senator McCarthy. One of them—Arthur Miller—seemed to feel that the American playwright could no longer speak freely, the other—oddly enough, James Thurber—that he could no longer even breathe freely—freely enough to relax and be funny.[1] Both statements have value as warnings; I cannot see that they have as yet much substance in fact. Satiric or other comedy may presuppose more freedom than at present exists in Russia; I cannot see—thinking of Aristophanes and Molière—that it presupposes more freedom than at present exists in America, even granting a harsh estimate of how much that is.[2] And in what sense have our playwrights lost their freedom of speech? It would, I suppose, be impossible for a Communist playwright to find backers for an openly Communist

1. "The constant open season on writers has seriously depressed literature in America. It has taken the exuberance and gaiety out of the theatre . . . Playwrights may come out of hiding and start working happily again if they hear the old reassuring sound of America laughing; but if the subpoenas for Hellman and Odets are the beginning of an endless probe of Broadway, then the American theatre cannot be saved and will die."—James Thurber in "Dark Suspicions," *The New York Times,* July 27, 1952.

2. Heine said: "It is certainly a mistake to attribute the sterility of the German Thalia to the lack of free air; or, if I may be allowed the frivolous word, to the lack of political freedom. That which is called political freedom is in no wise necessary to the prosperity of comedy. If one recalls Venice, where, in spite of the leaden chambers and the secret drownings, Goldoni and Gozzi created their masterpieces; or Spain, where, despite the absolutist axe and the orthodox stake, those delightful cloak and dagger pieces were devised."— *The French Stage.*

play, just as it would have been impossible for a Fascist playwright to find backers for an openly Fascist play at any time between 1930 and 1945. Even so, the only Communist play I know of during the past few years had a small New York production and full-scale productions in Iron Curtain countries which presumably pay royalties. Is the present plea for freedom of speech a plea for any opinions other than Communist opinions? Or is the complaint that any unorthodox opinion is dubbed Communist? If that's it, the unjustly accused playwright deserves our sympathy and help, like the unjustly accused actor and professor. What I cannot see is how dramaturgy suffers.

A radical playwright, in any case, can't have it both ways: he can't make his living by flinging accusations at established society and then scold society for taking his living away if it flings some accusations back. In the past, it has been very safe on Broadway to hold dangerous views, and the result has been a spate of easy virtue. The only playwright who could not have got his plays put on would have been the anti-liberal. On the Negro question, for example, Broadway has its own strict orthodoxy. The Broadway radical has been in fact one of the more pampered members of the community. Though an unpampered radical said, when a play of his was rejected, "Well, I don't expect them

to pay for their own liquidation," the pampered ones may be defined as those who expect just that.

In any event, we must look at a much longer span of time than Mr. Miller and Mr. Thurber were considering. The impression we have of "decline" over a period of five or even ten years is reversed as soon as one play we like comes along. I agree that *The Male Animal* is better than the comedies of recent seasons, but there may be a better one than *The Male Animal* at any moment (by Mr. Thurber, for example). Pondering the American theatre since 1900, one is bound to long for plays better than any on the whole record. Before 1918, after all, the American drama was almost moronic. The improvement in the Twenties was so great it rather naturally went to everyone's head. O'Neill was thought to have superseded Ibsen and to be comparable, rather, to Shakespeare and Aeschylus. I respect several of the critics who carried on in this way and I have been relieved to discover that, when challenged, they retract their hyperboles and hence call for no refutation from the rest of us. There was no Elizabethan Age, there were not even any Shaws, Chekhovs and Strindbergs, but there were the Provincetown, the Guild, the Group Theatre, the Mercury, the Federal Theatre. At last there were some playwrights, even if there could not, all at once, be a profession of playwriting. There were theatres with the idea of continuity in them. From this germ, if at all, must grow an acting profession.

And now what? Circumstances continue to be against the playwright. Production in New York grows more and more expensive, public abasement before the eight daily reporters more and more abject. The Administration of Eisenhower is not likely to restore a Federal Theatre which even a Democratic Congress let fall. The American National Theatre and Academy is interested, I am told, in decentralizing the theatre and depriving New York of its monopoly. Whether its leaders know how this can be done, or whether, if so, they can do it, is another matter. However, it is probably worth while to support ANTA; not knowing what "the one thing necessary" is, we must perforce try everything. Every effort in the direction of a professional theatre, a theatre with continuity, must be backed up.

Can our efforts succeed? The facts wouldn't lead one to expect so, nor have I (or other people, apparently) a convincing over-all plan for the conquest of the facts. I console myself, on the other hand, with the reflection that drama—drama of talent, let alone drama of genius—has not come in the past by prescription, nor was it predictable. The professions of playwriting and acting which

Shakespeare entered as a young man had not existed much more than a generation before him.
Dramatic history can be swift, especially when the
preparations have been made; and the activity of
1900–50 in America might certainly be regarded as
preparatory. What is more, if drama died easy, it
would already be dead. The art has a powerful
hold on quite a number of people, among whom I
count myself. And if now I seem to be working up
an optimistic peroration, I would ask: what *can* I
think? If you were a pterodactyl of the decadence,
no one could expect you to talk in the tone of
restrospective biology. Your business would be to
die; and you can die with all the more dignity if
you think you're not going to die at all.

(1953–54)

AFTERTHOUGHT, 1967

The penultimate paragraph of this essay seems
especially time-bound. Since 1953, much effort has
gone into the decentralization of the American
theatre, and there have been notable achievements
in San Francisco, Dallas, Minneapolis, Washington,
and elsewhere. On the very day when I read proof
of the present book, July 26, 1967, *The New York
Times* reported:

Is the Drama an Extinct Species?

Los Angeles, July 25.—The first permanent Federally subsidized professional theater in the United States, financed by nearly $1-million, was established here today . . .

Yet it would be premature to say that a completely new situation had defined itself or that my generalizations of 1953 now require radical revision. As far as New York is concerned, costs are now higher, even relative to the higher general cost of living. During the 1966–67 season, the number of daily reviewers got reduced to three: what difference this makes, if any, still remains to be seen.

THE
AMERICAN DRAMA
[1944–1954]

1 . THE ECONOMICS OF IT

IT COSTS anything from forty to a hundred and
fifty thousand dollars to put a play on Broadway.
It cost $23,000 to put on *Life With Father* in 1939,
and $85,000 to put on *Life With Mother* in 1948.
Mother cost three and a half times as much. One
could cite wider differences. A famous Saroyan
play was put on before the war for about $5,000. A
famous Tennessee Williams play was put on in
1953 for $115,000.[1] That is twenty-three times as

1. Extreme cases. *My Heart's in the Highlands* was done
only at special matinées. Few straight plays in 1953 cost as
much as *Camino Real*. Musicals, on the other hand, cost
much more: *Kismet* cost $400,000. There are further particu-
lars, highly relevant to this chapter, in two important
Harper's articles by John Houseman: "No Business Like
Show Business," September 1949, and "The Critics in the
Aisle Seats," October 1951.

much. It would take a more expert statistician than I to say what is the average increase since 1939. Place it anywhere you wish between three and a half and twenty-three, and you have an increase such as any business might find it hard to meet.

These figures help to explain the state of dramatic art better than any conceivable remarks about dramaturgy. However, instead of discussing union regulations, the "real estate situation," competition from movies and TV, I shall simply note the principal condition they impose on theatre—namely, that no play shall be performed unless a small group of wealthy men will bet on its having a long run. For it takes months of playing to capacity houses for investors to so much as get their money back.

What kind of play is the safest bet? No one quite knows, and that is perhaps the one happy aspect of the situation: think how dreadful it would be if we knew for certain that good plays always flop! Nevertheless, though no one lays claim to certitude, and an extraordinary number of hits are surprise hits, there *is* a general prejudice on Broadway against certain types of drama and in favor of others. Other things being equal, a play that can in any sense be defined as highbrow is considered a bad bet. It is not equally true that a play considered lowbrow is always considered a good bet. At this point, other criteria enter in. For example: all those who have opinions about plays seem to agree that one recent Broadway show, *The Fifth Season*, is an execrable play. Yet it was a hit; and its success was predicted by people with opinions, not about plays, but about garment workers, pretty girls, and Menasha Skulnik. A producer's job is not to judge plays but to "know the angles"—in more academic language, to know what criteria are relevant to success. That is, this *would* be his job, if it were possible. Since it has seemed to be impossible, what we witness is prejudice against so-called highbrow works and sheer guesswork among lowbrow works. "If only it were easier to tell good shit from bad shit," a producer said to me. We need not pity such a producer too much—we have our own troubles—but many of us do have some feeling about the prejudice against the so-called highbrow: we resent it. We have a prejudice against that prejudice.

I have simplified the producer-speculator's problem if I've suggested that he bets directly on the public's response. Actually, he doesn't ask about Tom, Dick and Harry but about Brooks Atkinson and Walter Kerr. "What will the critics think?" When the first performance is over, the producer presides over a dismal supper party till the small hours of the morning when the eight reviews are relayed to him by phone. If he has produced a serious play, and the reviewers don't like it, he is done for. If some of them like it, he is done for. Only if all of them write of it in a vein of corny exultation is he sure of a hit.

Many people still blame this state of affairs on the critics, but, as the latter are always pointing out, that is unfair: it isn't their fault if people take so much notice of them. And it is not true that they are unusually dogmatic men. On the contrary, one might more justly complain of some of them that they play the role of the crumply little man who apologizes for having an opinion at all. They make such admissions of ignorance that one might say their motto is: "I thank thee, God, for my humility."

Why does the New York public pay so much more attention to the newspaper critics than it used to? Is it the higher price of a ticket that makes the customer more cautious? Is caution the best description of credulous dependence on eight reporters? Or is such behavior a straw in some more horrible wind? A token of an abject reliance on pundits that brings us nearer to George Orwell's 1984?

The Fifth Season is a play that succeeded without the critics, as musicals and other light entertainments not seldom do. The paradox of the critics' position is that they completely control the serious drama which they hardly even claim to understand, while no one very much cares what they say of light entertainment which they are quite at home with. Where they have competence, they have no power, and vice versa.

I should not like to leave the subject of economics without admitting there are exceptions to the rule that no play shall be performed unless a small group of wealthy men will bet on its having a long run. There *is* a non-commercial theatre which has three great sources of income outside the box office: private philanthropy, the local community (or group philanthropy), and the state legislatures. That is: there *are* producers who will put on certain shows—with little or no hope of profit—because they like them; there are community theatres, such as those of Cleveland, Pasadena and Dallas; and there are the theatres of the great state universities supported by the taxpayer. Such are the American approaches to a subsidized theatre. (Even the Federal Theatre of 1936–1939 was not a state theatre in the European sense but a free-wheeling, hyper-American interpretation of a public relief program.)

Non-commercial theatres deserve all the encouragement we can give them except that of flattery.

The fact that we want to get more and more money for them is no reason for overlooking their present limitations. Let us admit that they are more often a provincial substitute for Broadway than an alternative to it. To call them collectively the Tributary Theatre is misleading. They do not pour their own waters into the larger stream. They are rather the Parasitic Theatre, drawing what little life they have from New York.

An extreme—if, therefore, special—case is the Summer Theatre, which manages to be considerably more hidebound than Broadway. In New York, an actor's name is seldom enough to draw an audience; on Cape Cod, nothing else matters. In New York, a "name" actor usually—not always—has also to be a good performer; in a summer theatre, any nincompoop from Hollywood will do. The formula is a movie star, even one who hasn't acted in twenty years, any old company, any old director, and any old hit play.

So if you come along with a new play which is not too easy or too stupid, which is not identical in pattern with a dozen accepted hits, it may be hard to get it produced on Broadway but it may well be even harder to get it produced anywhere else. A corollary of this fact is that many plays that are worth seeing are done in New York and never sent out on the road afterward. The most recent works.

of Arthur Miller and Tennessee Williams are examples.

There is also the matter of how the plays are done. But before I tell what I have seen, I should like to describe my angle of vision.

2. THE CRITICIZING OF IT

There is daily reviewing, and there is weekly reviewing. Most of the daily reviewers are weekly reviewers too, inasmuch as they add a Sunday article to their daily notices. But in principle daily and weekly reviewing differ. The daily reviewer is a reporter setting down right after the performance the responses of an "ordinary" playgoer. It is a very hard job—as reporting on anything, a football match or a street accident, is hard: it calls for a more observant eye and a more fluent pen than most of us possess. The weekly reviewer * has the privilege of more time both to write and do his homework. And his aim is different. On most magazines the task he is called on to perform is dual: he has to judge the show as an expert on shows

---

* The reader may need reminding at this point of the date of this essay (1954) at which time I was weekly dramatic critic for *The New Republic.*

(not an average playgoer) and he has to entertain his readers with his thinking on and around the subject. Since the fate of a play in New York has been settled before the weekly magazine reaches the stands, weekly criticism has no immediate effect. To the weekly critic this seems both good and bad: it is a relief to know that you aren't doing anyone out of a living when you pan a performance, and on the other hand it is depressing to feel that what you say has no practical importance. I sometimes feel my reviews have been dropped into a bottomless well, that they are contributions to a discussion that never takes place.

Even if I feel sure I am writing for a reader, it is hard for me to know his identity. The weekly reviewer has to satisfy New Yorkers who have seen the play or will see it; he is also read by many outside New York who will not see it. Ninety per cent of *New Republic* sales are outside Manhattan. But then the Broadway audience is to a large extent composed of out-of-towners. So I have no idea what proportion of my hypothetical readers sees the shows. I find the thought of two distinct types of readers rather disturbing. I intend each article for both "inside" theatre people and for non-theatre people on the outside; yet there is some evidence that the former find my pieces too full of known information while the latter find them over-allusive and obscure. I should perhaps give the job up as hopeless but for the example of Stark Young who performed it so well for over twenty years. His procedure was simple: he set down what was of interest to him and left readers to fend for themselves.

The New Republic has a tradition in dramatic criticism. My two [2] predecessors on the magazine—Stark Young and Harold Clurman—stand apart from most of their colleagues in being less concerned with journalism than with theatre. Both have worked on the other side of the footlights. The personal relations with actors which such an interest entails set the critic problems of tact that are susceptible of no perfect solution. It is impossible for him to be both as frank as he should be and as discreet as he should be, as ruthless as he should be and as charitable as he should be. He is always either bowing and scraping or bending over backward. He knows too much. On the other hand, very few people have ever learned much about acting and production from seats out front after the rehearsal period is over. These are arts you learn as playwright, actor, director, designer, not as theatre-goer, nor yet as critic.

2. Strictly speaking, three; and the third, Irwin Shaw, has also had a lot of theatre experience; but he stayed with *The New Republic* only a few months.

Whatever a man's estimate of the total intelligence of drama critics, high or low, he cannot fail to notice that—except for a Young or a Clurman—they know far less about acting and directing than about literature. Which is another funny thing about this remarkable class of men. They know something of literature though they are anti-literary; they are pro-theatrical but know little of acting. And so, as was noted above, a mediocre performance of a mediocre play is often greeted as a magnificent performance of a bad play. A brash actor who ruins a play will not be found out. He may very well be praised. The ruin is blamed on the playwright.

This scolding of the reviewers leads to my next topic:

3. THE STAGING OF IT

Nowhere more than in stage design is the matter of expense the decisive one. America spends a lot on stage design and doesn't get very much for its money. Costs are so high that many of the best ideas have to be dropped as too expensive. This is the main fact to consider in making any comparison with the German or Russian stage. Producers breathe a sigh of relief if they are assured that a play can be done with one set. So we get stereotypes. The chief old-fashioned one is the stage drawing room with its familiar rows of bookshelves full of unread books, the couch here, the armchair there, the staircase, the door, the piano and of course the phone. The chief new-fashioned one is the interior-and-exterior-combined (*Death of a Salesman, Rose Tattoo, Streetcar*), of which the porch-and-surroundings is a variant (*All My Sons, Picnic*). Some sets of these two types have been very fine pieces of composition, but the possibilities of variation are limited; and the alternatives to the standard modern patterns seem also to run to type. Thus there is the gorgeous-gaudy show, lowbrow in musical comedies, highbrow in opera; brains and ingenuity and a certain lush taste go into these things; but no style is achieved. Then there is Shakespeare with platforms and drapes. Though the scheme has its points, they are not as many as at one time was expected. The same could be said of that more recent scheme: central staging.

If we look at the designs of Christian Bérard of Paris, Teo Otto of Zurich, or Caspar Neher of Salzburg, we find more of a style—more of a realized modernity—than even the most brilliant men are giving us here. We don't give our men enough practice, and we don't give them wide enough powers; so they find themselves caught between musical comedy with its miles of gaudy, old-fashioned scenery and the one-set play with its inevitable porch or its inevitable bookcase. We have fine craftsmen, but they work under restrictions both artistic and technical that prevent their giving any adequate account of themselves. Ask why, and we are back again with economics.[3]

In this brief survey I shall not attempt to speak of directing: acting is more important. And, at that, directing today is less the mounting of giant spectacles, the marshalling of crowds, the unfurling of scenery, than it is the training of actors. Because we have no national theatre and no network of repertory theatres, we offer our young actors far too little either of variety or continuity. Still, certain remedial measures have been taken. The creation of the Group Theatre was one such measure—back in the Thirties. It was followed by the creation of the Actors' Studio in the Forties. In these organizations, a new generation of American actors has been trained, and a new type of Ameri-

3. There are other resources we don't use beside the human ones. I am not equipped to expound the theory and practice of George C. Izenour of Yale. But it is pretty clear that his researches have rendered the switchboard—and therefore much of the stagecraft—of all our theatres quite obsolete . . .

can actor has evolved. The easiest way of telling the layman about the new acting is to inform him that he has seen it in *Death of a Salesman* or *A Streetcar Named Desire*. It is a deliberate American alternative to the elocutionary "style acting" that we import from England. It seizes on the nervous excitement of American life—healthy or unhealthy—and communicates it. It makes older-fashioned acting seem stilted, slow and emptily declamatory. I never felt this so sharply as when seeing *Tea and Sympathy* as directed by the head of the Studio, Elia Kazan, the night after a Margaret Webster production (*The Strong Are Lonely*). It was like finding myself on an express train after sitting yawning in the waiting room. On the other hand, reviewing plays which are acted by members of the Studio, I have had frequent occasion to note the narrow scope of the newer acting. It almost seems limited to the portrayal of violent and neurasthenic types.

Two other kinds of acting are expertly practiced in America. The first is musical comedy acting, which includes singing and perhaps dancing. The second is light comedy acting. The lay public scarcely distinguishes the two; yet the distinction is in fact a fairly broad one. Musical comedy technique starts—I think—with song: not so much with the music as such, not with singing, but with

the art of performing a song, handing it to the
public by means of singing, half-singing, interpo-
lated speaking and pantomime. Then the postures
and gestures—the whole art of putting a song
over—extend themselves even into the parts of musical comedy which are not sung; so that, if you see
a musical comedy actor in a straight play, you say:
it seems as if he's always just going to sing. His
bouncy manner, the little springs he takes from
one foot to the other, the way he keeps lifting his
arms in salutation or extending his fist in a
punch—all these things come from the pantomime
of a singer. It is quite a jump from this to light
comedy—from, say, Alfred Drake in *Kismet* to Elliott Nugent in *The Male Animal*. Light comedy
has an inner connection with broader forms (like
the musical) but conceals it; and that is the joke.
There is a portentous pretense of grave reality.
The vitality of a performance in light comedy depends on the degree of tension between the seem-
ing reality and the concealed madness. The comic
climaxes are reached when gay and furious imps of
folly come surging up into a hitherto decorous
situation. Any drunk scene is likely to be a simple
instance of the pattern; and, in a sense, all light
comedy is drunken comedy.

Domestic drama, musical comedy, light
comedy—these are what American actors are

trained to perform. They aren't all of theatre. If we want to do Shakespeare or Wilde or Shaw or Eliot we are in trouble. British actors are called upon, and—to the extent that Actors' Equity lets them in—a provisional solution is arrived at. In the long run American actors have got to be trained to do these other kinds of work themselves. Shakespeare in particular is an author each country has to study and interpret for itself. The American Shakespeare might even be better than the British; at any rate, it would be different.

4. THE WRITING OF IT

Many of the most serviceable scripts of the past ten years have been in the less serious categories—musical and light comedy. The book of a musical is seldom impressive of itself; you go to musical comedy for everything except the words; yet, behind the music and dancing, the book may be efficiently doing its job.

Light comedy tends to have witty words wittily spaced out and arranged. If one were asked: what is the best American play? one might not have the temerity to say *The Male Animal* or *Born Yesterday,* yet they are better plays than most of those that have a higher reputation; and certainly, if you want a good evening, a light comedy is nowadays more likely to supply it than the so-called serious drama. During the 1953-4 season, for instance, one of the dullest evenings was an earnest treatise on the United Nations called *The Prescott Proposals.* One of the brightest was a joke about a comic-strip artist called *King of Hearts.*

Even inferior plays in the lighter vein often have something rather striking about them. It was agreed that a play called *Men of Distinction* was one of the very bad plays of the 1952-3 season; yet there was something very good about it. In fact, it had one virtue of such a provoking sort that not only the deficiency of the play but also its merit militated against success. This virtue was a cocky satirical humor totally unsoftened by sentimentality. There being no nice character in the play "to root for," you were unable to detach yourself from the non-nice characters. What made matters worse, they seemed nice. One of them was a Harvard man as personable and charming as Harvard's representatives on Broadway, Brooks Atkinson and John Mason Brown. But he was a pimp. (I said at the beginning that the fate of a play at the hands of the reviewers was unpredictable; *Men of Distinction* is an exception.)

Turning to plays of more serious intent, I do not

33

know which are the best of the past ten years. *The Iceman Cometh* would be a candidate, *The Autumn Garden* another, *The Country Girl* a third, yet all three are in the nature of postscripts to a communication written in an earlier decade. I prefer to pick out for discussion plays which belong more exclusively to the period under review. Of course they have traditions behind them—two traditions in particular: that of the social drama and that of the psychological "mood play."

It is agreed that the most interesting social dramas of the period are *Death of a Salesman* and *The Crucible.* Sidney Kingsley's version of *Darkness at Noon* is just as skillful a piece of craftsmanship, is in subject matter much closer to the center of social conflict and makes a much clearer statement, but, for all the exciting bits that are its component parts, it is not quite a satisfying play. One reason for this is that the statement it makes is not only clear but obvious, not challengingly a little ahead of public opinion but boringly a little behind it. Why pay five dollars to be told that Communism * is unpleasant and immoral?

Maybe some people wish to. In that case, I shift my ground and say they shouldn't. We shouldn't

---

* The reader is again reminded of the date of this piece —1953-4—at which time Communism was monolithic and Stalinist.

go to the theatre to have our already inflated self-righteousness further blown up by ritual denunciation of an acknowledged villain's villainy. The theatre should be less serious than that—or more so. It should be a place either of innocent frivolity—or of moral responsibility. There is an unending war to fight in our theatre against those who are frivolous without being innocent and moralistic without being moral.

But not many people did wish to see *Darkness at Noon.*

They saw Arthur Miller's plays. Why? How could Mr. Miller's plays be more interesting if, as I have said, they are no better in craftsmanship, are less clear in meaning and further from the center of social struggle?

At the center of things nowadays is the matter of Communism. Mr. Kingsley put his play together to say so, and the play falls a little flat because we hold the truth of the proposition to be self-evident. What does Mr. Miller say about Communism? He doesn't mention it; yet the word—spoken or not—is likely to be at the center of a discussion of Mr. Miller. Now which fact is more important—that Mr. Miller doesn't mention Communism—or that you don't discuss him without mentioning it?

Suppose we ask in any group of liberal intellectuals: do *All My Sons* and *Death of a Salesman* present a Marxian analysis of American society? Or: does *The Crucible* say that American Communists should not be investigated? Some will answer yes, others will answer no; a certain heat and anxiety will get into the discussion; and a very vocal group will resent the fact that the questions have been asked in the first place. Mr. Miller may hold such and such a position, but, we shall be told, it is not—definitely not—playing fair to say so. In short, we encounter certain ambiguities and we find that these ambiguities have a strong emotional resonance among our fellows.

What is the nature of this resonance? What would explain so large an investment of emotion in Mr. Miller's plays on the part of those who don't wish us to ask questions? Take *The Crucible.* It is a play in which Mr. Miller complains that the accuser is always considered holy, the accused guilty. We think of McCarthyism; and we think of it again when we find that Mr. Miller's story is about a witch hunt. What is unusual about Mr. Miller's treatment of McCarthyism? One thing above all others: that he sets up as the offense which the seventeenth-century McCarthys accused people of an offense which it is impossible to commit: the practice of magic. If to the McCarthyites (of both periods) an accused man is almost automatically guilty, to Mr. Miller he is almost automatically innocent. If one were to ask: what fantasy would give most perfect expression to a Communist's feeling of innocence in the face of McCarthyism? one couldn't do better than reply: Mr. Miller's story. Mr. Miller has missed the essence of our political situation. He has thereby missed a more interesting dramatic situation. But he has hit upon a wish-fulfilling fantasy that, conceivably, has a stronger appeal than either; and with it he has soothed the bad conscience of a generation.

Just as the good liberal is not supposed to mention Communism when discussing Mr. Miller in general, so he is not supposed to mention Communism—or McCarthyism—when discussing *The Crucible* in particular. The production of the play was preceded by a quarrel between Mr. Miller and Elia Kazan. Mr. Kazan went on record as a former Communist and named some of his former comrades; in the last scene of *The Crucible,* Mr. Miller presented a man whose dignity consists in refusing to talk under pressure of the investigators. But that one is not supposed to find any connection between that scene and the Kazan incident I discovered when I tried to get some remarks on the subject into a liberal journal. The play, I was told, was about the seventeenth century. I gathered that, though I could have criticized Mr. Kazan's attitude, I mustn't criticize Mr. Miller's.

It is no business of mine—in this context—that Mr. Miller may be wrong. I am contending that he is ambiguous, and this in a way that would amount to trickery were it deliberate. I assume that, like the rest of us, he doesn't deliberately deceive others but involuntarily deceives himself. What gives this fact public importance is that so many of our fellow citizens want to share these particular self-deceptions with him. Let me illustrate. Indignation is Mr. Miller's stock in trade: his writing has Attack.[4] But what is he attacking? And is he really attacking it? "He's attacking the American way of life," says someone. "Why, nothing of the sort," says someone else. "He shows great sympathy for it." The punch is threatened; and then pulled. We are made to feel the boldness of the threat; then we are spared the violence of the blow. Now isn't this particular ambiguity strikingly characteristic of that large wing of the liberal movement which has been overawed by Communism? They admire the audacity of Communism all the more because they don't share it. They admire fearless outspokenness above all things; yet if outspokenness is actually to be feared, they fear

4. "Daring is of the essence. Its very nature is incompatible with an undue affection for moderation, respectability, even fairness, and responsibleness."—Arthur Miller in "Many Writers: Few Plays," *The New York Times*, August 10, 1952.

it; [5] and choose fearless silence. *The Crucible* is a play for people who think that pleading the Fifth Amendment is not only a white badge of purity but also a red badge of courage.

Another habit of the quasi-liberal mind has been to say that of course so-and-so is not a Communist and yet, when it turns out that so and so is or was a Communist, to register no dismay, not even surprise. Of course he wasn't a Communist; but, if he was, so what? This ambiguity has been given rather powerful expression by Lillian Hellman in *The Children's Hour* which was revived in the 1952–3 season with changes expressly calculated to suggest the play's relevance to McCarthyism. The play can be translated into political terms as follows. Someone is accused of Communism and says, "How absurd, I never heard of Communism, this is a witch hunt, my accuser is psychotic," and you believe him and your heart bleeds. Then this someone says: "Well, maybe I do carry a party card, either it's all this red-baiting that's driven me into the arms of Communism or, well, being a Communist isn't as bad as you as-

5. "But we have an atmosphere of dread just the same, an unconsciously—or consciously—accepted party line, a sanctified complex of moods and attitudes, proper and improper. If nothing else comes of it one thing surely has—it has made it dangerous to dare, and worse still, impractical." —Arthur Miller, *ibid.*

sume. The social system *is* pretty terrible. You admit *that,* I suppose? I'm going to kill myself in a minute. My death will make you feel awful. Please be indignant about it."

The Crucible and *The Children's Hour* represent a type of liberalism that has been dangerous and is now obsolescent. *Darkness at Noon* is more defensible on political or even moral grounds; yet it fails to stir us for reasons I have tried to state. If these are our best social plays, one wonders what the future holds for the genre. Shall we ever have a social drama with the purity and force of *The Power of Darkness* or *The Lower Depths?* [6]

Perhaps the creative forces in America are no longer running into political art. More prominent, certainly, in our theatre than social drama is the "mood play." I am referring to the school of playwrights—the only American school of playwrights—which is headed by Tennessee Williams and includes Carson McCullers, William Inge and Jane Bowles. In a recent book, *Playwright at Work,* John van Druten has hailed this school as a fine new drama gloriously superseding the old in much the

6. A couple of shows from the 1953–4 season—*End as a Man* and *The Caine Mutiny Court Martial*—suggest that the New Conservatism may have a vogue in the theatre under the slogan: Respect Authority. Both shows have force; but it is scarcely the force of their message; and both are as impure and equivocal as any liberal effort.

same way as William Archer hailed the school of
Ibsen half a century ago. One has one's doubts.

The moral weakness of the social drama is that
it scorns or neglects the self. Liberal idealism of
the sort I have described springs from fear—even
hatred—of the self. The new psychological drama,
school of Williams, is equal and opposite. It
springs from fear of the Other, of society, of the
world, and from preoccupation with the self. Now
art that doesn't spring from the whole man but
from one side of him tends, I think, not to become
art at all but to remain neurotic or quasi-neurotic
fantasy. The archetype of political fantasy is, perhaps, an imagined oration to a Congress of the
Party of your dreams. The archetype of non-
political fantasy is an imagined confession to a
psychoanalyst. Are the attitudes we find embodied
in dramatic fantasies of either kind any more adequate for good drama then they are for the good
life?

However this may be, one can certainly take
exception to the view of form and structure implied in the new works and openly championed by
their admirers. Mr. van Druten puts this view in a
nutshell when he says he'd like a play to be all
atmosphere and no plot. He says he finds inspiration and guidance in *The Member of the Wedding,*
The Glass Menagerie and *The Cherry Orchard.*

These are not plays I should wish to attack: one is a masterpiece, all are good evenings of theatre. However, none of them seems to me as mysteriously structureless as Mr. van Druten implies. Perhaps Plot is the name he gives to a structure he finds bad or at least obtrusive? Or is it just that he enjoys economy of means and the audacity with which a playwright can push big, tempting events into the background? Chekhov could push a duel-to-the-death off into the wings while the center of the stage is occupied by someone reading a newspaper and whistling a tune. Mrs. McCullers kills off the little cousin between scenes of *Member of the Wedding*. This is not to say that either Chekhov or Mrs. McCullers has no plot, though Mr. van Druten admits that *Member of the Wedding* is open to criticism on the grounds that its action is too slender; which is to say it has a plot but not a very big—or perhaps a very good?—plot. Only by the beauty of the lines, the addition of music, romantic lighting and the personality of two fine actresses could the play command a whole evening. It is a little story prolonged by theatrical legerdemain.

Picnic I do not know in the state the author left it but only in its final state as directed by Joshua Logan. Mr. Inge clearly contributed admirable character sketches, group portraits, local color, anecdotes. . . . Can one venture to say that it took the showmanship of a musical-comedy director to give *Picnic* the size of a complete show?

Jane Bowles' *In the Summer House* posed a similar problem but met with a different solution. This play had rather a *succès d'estime* in New York largely, it is said, because of a performance by Judith Anderson which the critics called magnificent. Magnificent or not, this performance had little relation to the character Mrs. Bowles conceived. Yet—and this is my point—I don't know that the play would have stood up by itself. It needed a buttress made of harder material; and *that* Miss Anderson certainly is.

I am not interested in establishing that any of the plays I mention is weak but only that it might have been stronger had the author not followed current fashion and assumed he could get along without the traditional kinds of support. I do not mean that a bad playwright could ever become a good one by dropping one attitude and taking up another—only that mistaken notions can hamper a good writer. (I assume that writers we take an interest in are to some extent good.) Nor am I saying that Mr. van Druten's book is having a bad influence. Rather, it sums up—and is influenced by—the view of drama which the more sophisticated people in the theatre had already come to hold.

This view is largely false. Chekhov's plays (for

example) have a cast-iron structure, only it is concealed, like the girders of a modern building. Tennessee Williams (for another example) is no model of plotlessness. The fashionable components of plot may have shifted since Archer's day but *A Streetcar Named Desire* has a strong, straightforward story, organized on principles that would be familiar to any earlier generation. What is the play in fact but the American version of *Miss Julie?* Even *The Glass Menagerie* has what I would call a plot. In short, I cannot see that the plays Mr. van Druten admires were constructed according to the theory he expounds; on the contrary, they seem to me to have merit insofar as they contravene this theory.

5. CRITICIZING THE CRITICIZING OF IT

Ça commence à bien faire...

Having stated where I think our playwrights are going wrong, I should like to end by saying where criticism, including of course my own, may go wrong. I shall go wrong if I imagine that the playwright needs me to tell him what to do. Drama criticism is not a disguised and prolonged course in playwriting. If a man can write plays, he doesn't need a critic to push his pen. If he can't, he doesn't need a critic to dig his grave.

A critic is only a judge. A judge doesn't help you to commit your crime or even to abstain from committing it. His verdict—too late to influence the actions under consideration—has value, if at all, not for the prisoner, but for society at large. I implied earlier that the drama critic mustn't be modest and pretend he's the man in the street. (Between aisle seat and desk chair he knows only the inside of a taxi.) I am insisting now that he also lay no claim to direct influence on writers. If by chance he does exert such an influence, and it is salutary, so much the better; this is service over and above the call of duty. All he regularly and imperatively does is help to create the climate of opinion in which the playwrights live.

That is no small matter. The cultural air has often become oppressive. And it has done so, not when criticism was keen and demanding, but when it was non-existent. One writer who resented the power of critics got himself made propaganda minister and legislated criticism out of existence, substituting *Kunstbetrachtung*—that is, reportage and eulogy. This was Goebbels. In Russia, critical analysis is dismissed as formalistic. A writer is praised as a yes-man or silenced as a saboteur.

Though the direct influence of dramatic criticism is small, its indirect effect could be considerable. Bernard Shaw stated the converse of this proposition when he spoke of the "ruinous privilege of exemption from vigilant and implacable criticism." There is, of course, a converse of this converse: that the right to criticize enjoins the duties of vigilance and implacability.

(1953–54)

WHAT IS THEATRE?

TO WRITE theatre reviews is worse than walking on eggs; it is to walk on live bodies and make them bleed. The critic's comments may be far less harsh than those that are heard at every cocktail party in New York. But, while the party-goers only commit the venial sin of stabbing their fellow men in the back, and their victims will never find out who did it, the critic commits the unpardonable crime of striking right between the eyes and taking the responsibility in public. His victims know whom to hate and receive abundant sympathy to their face from those who, behind their back, agree with the critic. I sometimes feel that theatre reviewing is the art of making enemies and failing to influence people.

Nonetheless, I have gone on reviewing in the only way I know how. To those who consider it an entirely pointless or wrong way I can say nothing, but I should like to remonstrate with those who remonstrate with me for being what they consider unnecessarily harsh and highhanded, who write letters asking if I never, never realize that I might be mistaken, and try to get under my moral guard by demanding which do I want to do, *en*courage people, or *dis*courage them, help theatre or hinder it? For the fact that a critic may be wrong (just like the critics of a critic) is no reason for him, especially as he thinks, poor man, that he is right, not to express his views as clearly as he can or even to abstain, in so doing, from the practice of all the arts of persuasion, which include every kind of civilized aggression from gentle irony to clamorous invective.

It is understandable that in moments of anger or wounded feelings, any one of us should call on heaven or the government forthwith and forever to abolish criticism. Naturally, each one of us taken separately, and speaking strictly for himself, does not want to be criticized: he wants to be praised. "For myself, praise; for the other two billion inhabitants of the world, criticism"—it isn't a practical proposition, so the thwarted egoist reluctantly agrees to let everyone else be praised too. To an extraordinary extent, the frustrated artist Goebbels did substitute eulogy for criticism in Germany. And in America there is a current of anti-intellectualism which can grow, whenever we don't watch it, into an irresistible tide. That is why I feel that the energy of men of good will is less well spent asking critics not to criticize than it would be in asking the community at large to hold on to its critics in the face of totalitarianism and the psychology of what David Riesman calls an "other-directed" [1] generation.

This applies, also, to the question of discouragement. Certainly, I, like anyone else, am discouraged, sometimes very painfully so, when my work is unfavorably criticized. I am afraid I take criticism seriously. Suppose there were no serious criticism. Then the praise of so-called critics could not be taken seriously, and by that token could not be encouraging. When all plays are praised, a good review will mean precisely nothing; some reviews are encouraging only because others are not. Criticized artists learn to take the rough with the

1. ". . . a social character whose conformity is insured by their tendency to be sensitized to the expectations and preferences of others." "What is common to all the other-directed people is that their contemporaries are the source of direction for the individual." "While all people want and need to be liked by some of the people some of the time, it is only the modern other-directed types who make this their chief source of direction and chief area of sensitivity." ". . . the other-directed person, though he has his eye very much on the Joneses, aims to keep up with them not so much in external details as in the quality of his inner experience."—From *The Lonely Crowd: a Study of the Changing American Character,* by David Riesman.

smooth, and my experience in this field gives me the impression that the generality of them have done so. Those who cannot "take it" are most commonly not those who are starved for want of a little recognition but those who have been spoiled with over-praise. Our culture over-sells every product. Reputations are never simply high, they are hopelessly over-inflated. One of a critic's main jobs is to prick balloons.

We believe in freedom of discussion, but do we believe in discussion? In the theatre, the phenomenon is almost unheard of, for one cannot describe as discussion either the ballyhoo of the publicity men or that grandiose gab by which certain theatre people try to make their next show sound like the second coming of the Lord. Yet criticism is discussion before it is either praise or condemnation.

I am sometimes thought to be so much in love with French and German theatre that I automatically dislike anything English or American. But countries are no more equal theatrically than, say, in their military establishments. Certain German cities and one French city have theatrical traditions that are not rivaled in many other places, certainly not in London or New York. We should be able to face a fact like that without contemplating suicide—or even emigration.

Take this matter of criticism *qua* discussion. When a Mauriac or a Sartre brings out a new play in Paris, it is discussed. Catholics present the Catholic point of view, Communists present the Communist point of view, every school of opinion presents its credentials. In New York, on the other hand, we like to "keep our religion out of it"—a Catholic critic would blush if anyone discovered that he went to church. We also like to "keep our politics out of it." And, consequently, there is a single political orthodoxy on Broadway, a liberalism so hazy and insubstantial that it can be shared by Communists and Republicans; and we go to political plays to make such epoch-making discoveries as that we like Negroes, dislike anti-Semites, and wish our country both to win the war and be nice to the natives.

We do have controversial plays, but not even the author expects there to be any controversy about them: he is only affronted that anyone should not find his work to be all that is noble and of good report. *The Crucible,* one of the most controversial plays of this decade, aroused very little controversy. As far as the New York press is concerned, I don't recall that anyone took issue with Mr. Miller except an editorial writer in the *Post.* And when Herman Wouk sailed into Broadway on the Caine, with some very high explosive politics in the cargo, one columnist, Mr. Arthur Schlesinger, said something about it, also in the *Post*. But, both times, the *Post's* dramatic critic was keeping his fingers out of politics—and out of discussion.

This season (1955–56) we have had, in Anouilh's *The Lark*, a presentation of the trial of Joan of Arc wanton enough in its anti-Catholic bias to make any fair-minded non-Catholic join the faithful, if not in protest, at least in debate. Yet, though the Catholic Bishop of Worcester saw the point, a large part of the Catholic public has accepted the play, being so secularized that it doesn't know the enemy when it sees him; like so many other sections of the population, it is in no position to discuss the issues. And the issues were not discussed, except in the cloisters of *Commonweal* and *The New Republic*.

"We don't discuss it" used to be something parents said about sex. Now that sex is discussed more than anything else, perhaps we should expect various other subjects to become unmentionable. Will theatre be one of them? Will playwriting be something one does behind barred doors and prefers not to talk about? That wouldn't really be any worse than the present situation in which discussion is limited to the oohing and aahing of routine eulogy and the tsk tsk tsk of routine disparagement. The proudest task dramatic criticism could propose for itself in this place at this time would be to replace animal noises with rational discourse.

But before this can be done, we need to examine our preconceptions. If so much of my criticism, or yours, is complaint that artists have missed the target, we have obviously been making assumptions as to what the target is. Destructive criticism, in fact, is justified only as springing from love of the object missed just as surely as eulogy is justified by love of the object attained. Even if our aim is only to criticize the critic, we need to know what the object is that he loves and precisely what it is *about* this object that inspires such love.

In the rest of this essay, I am going to state, as fully as I can in the space, what it is about theatre that I respect, admire and love. Possibly this procedure will confer some incidental benefits. Not least because we cannot remove a critic's prejudices, it is good to be able to see exactly what they are. Though, in the light of this confession, some of my judgments may seem less plausible than ever, it is my hope that others may begin to acquire a certain plausibility and that what appeared unnecessarily harsh and high-handed may be, at least partly, justified by the thought, the sentiment, or the attitude behind it.

What is the essence of theatre and its interest for us? What is the heart of the matter? Many, we know, have been stage-struck, but what was it, exactly, that struck them? Many have been more than stage-struck: they have emerged from the trance and given a lifetime of back-breaking labor to this singular institution. Many have suffered bitter poverty on its account, and bitterer humiliation, for worse than the constant economic hardships of theatre are the equally constant blows inflicted on everyone's self-respect. What is this art that exacts so high a price? Many have written about it, enthusiastically announcing their own view of it and opposing all other views witheringly, banteringly or even inarticulately. What is the *it* that arouses their enthusiasm, and the misconception of which makes them so scornful, so skittish or so hesitant?

Well, there's something about the theatre, one starts to say, before becoming uncomfortably aware how little one is adding to the store of knowledge.

There's something about a soldier
There's something about a soldier
There's something about a soldier that is fine,
fine, fine.

And if we cannot quite say why, let us at least try to say what.

To begin with, the theatre is a place. This place, in all known forms, sets up such a vibration in those who frequent it that certain properties roughly suggested by the term magic are invariably attributed to the building itself. In our epoch, for example, how many journalists, and even college freshmen, have mentioned the expectant lull when the lights dim, and the thrill when the curtain rises! This, you say, may be partly a matter of audience psychology. It remains true that the paraphernalia of the theatre has of itself remarkable suggestive power. Even when no audience is present, even when the stage is bare of scenery and the brick wall at the rear is exposed, the curious machine retains an insidious attraction. No more than a human being does a theatre necessarily lose its fascination by taking its clothes off. Pirandello obviously had been struck by that fact before he wrote *Six Characters in Search of an Author;* and also by the fact that the procedures of theatre carry a similar "magic." Rationally speaking, the rehearsal doings of actors and stage staff alike are either so sensible as to be rather dull or so foolish and anachronistic as to be contemptible. To know how the dullness and contemptibility are avoided and transcended would be to have solved the mystery of the theatre as a place.

If there is something about the place, there is something, too, about its inhabitants, the actors. I have not spoken of the merits of one building as against another, nor do I have in mind the merits of one actor as against another. There is something about the actor as such, about the mere fact of impersonation: there is a "magic" to this too. Various accounts have been given of the origin of such activity; various theories have been advanced to explain its continued and universal appeal. The fact itself is unequivocal. A child loves to dress up in grandmother's bonnet and feathers. Grownups go to carnivals and fancy-dress balls. To give the greatest possible effect to his story, the raconteur adds mimicry to narrative. Some primitive people believe that they can appease the gods by dressing up in certain ways; some non-primitive people believe they can cure neuroses by a form of charade or group impersonation which they have christened psycho-drama. A famous young actor was recently quoted by *The New York Times* as saying: "To me acting is the most logical way for people's neuroses to manifest themselves." I see no reason to believe him and several reasons for disbelieving him, yet I'm sure his heart was in the right place. He wanted to say something definitive when all he really sensed was that there's something about an actor.

There is something about an audience—that is, about a group of people in close physical proximity, with their faces all pointing one way, and their attention—their eyes, ears, hearts and minds— focused upon a single object. There is something about ceasing to be merely an *I* and becoming, under such circumstances, in this *place,* before that *actor,* a part of a *we.* There is something about the cosiness and sociability [2] of the whole physical setup. And possibly—though one hesitates to believe it—there is something about its uncosiness, unsociability and positive discomfort. The lack of knee room, the pest of people pushing past and, in New York, the ban on smoking, the absence of bars, the shortage of lobby space—such things lend weight to the occasion. Again, whatever the explanation, the fact is familiar: an experience is changed by being shared in such company in such a manner.

The extreme and notorious cases of audience psychology are cases of hysterics and swooning and the premature delivery of babies. But if we judge theatre merely by the *degree* of effect, then the best

2. ". . . the New York theatre-goer . . . can step into almost any theatre lobby with that sense of virtuous expectation, of responsibility and enlightenment, that the drama peculiarly awakes and that makes the theatre for New York what the café is for Paris, a pleasure and also a pride, a habit and a ritual, a diversion and a duty. To the extent that America has any communal life at all, it is centered in the New York theatre; here is the last refuge of sociability and humanism."—*Sights and Spectacles* by Mary McCarthy.

theatrical entertainment is a revivalist meeting or a political rally. In dramatic art proper, we are more concerned with moderate responses—with the fact, for example, that the joke *I* imperceptibly smile at alone in my study, *we* perceptibly grin at, we perhaps all "roar" at, in the theatre.

What's the matter, are we drunk? Boastful—wishing to show off our sociability? Polite—as one would laugh more loudly at a joke made by the president of the board? The less respectable motives no doubt enter in, as we are so directly under the noses of our fellow men, so mercilessly exposed and therefore bound to be on our "best" behavior; but is it not chiefly the atmosphere of a full theatre, the psychology of *we,* that has put us at our ease, and caused a great deal of good feeling to pour out of us that normally we would suppress? That is, if we felt it in the first place; for much of the good feeling is created by the occasion, by the psychology of *we.* Or perhaps, more accurately still, while initiated by the *actor* and the *place,* such feeling is constantly *increased* by the occasion, by the psychology of *we.* One speaks of "infectious enthusiasm," and the enjoyment of an audience is a positive contagion. The Puritans were wrong to call the theatre a scarlet woman; they would have been less wrong had they called theatregoing a scarlet fever. We acknowledge freely enough, I believe, that men go to football matches to share the orgiastic experience of communal waving, shoving, cheering and yelling. The orgiastic character of theatregoing is no longer overt, but surely it is one of the first things to take into account if we try to explain why anyone would pass up all the alternatives—especially TV at home and the movies on the corner—and go through hail and snow to an expensive but uncomfortable seat in an inconvenient building called a legitimate theatre. Fine word, "legitimate"! To think of the little thrillers they put on there, that would yield in the movies a non-stop feature of at most ninety minutes, and on TV at most an hour program with interspersed commercials! In what one is tempted to call this bastard of a legitimate theatre such items are stretched out for over two hours by the surely illegitimate device of lengthy intermissions during which there is no bar or restaurant to go to and only a grossly overcrowded lobby to smoke in.

What assets has the theatre got, to offset its appalling liabilities? Clearly, the *place,* the *actor* and the psychology of *we.* "But the movies have all three," counters someone. "For how could you have a film without a place to show it in, actors to play in it, and a crowd to see it?" Ah yes, but there is a "short" in that electrical system. No current flows from celluloid to audience—or, at any rate, no current flows from audience to celluloid. In the movie theatre, we can watch a story and we can admire many things that actors do, but we cannot be caught up in a flow of living feeling that passes from actor to audience and from the audience back again to the actor. In the movies, Shirley Booth may smile, and you may smile back at her; but she can scarcely catch your returning smile and toss it back again or change it and give it back in the form of a sob or a catch in the throat. Yet such are the dynamics of theatre. And, rightly or wrongly, there are people who undertake the trip to the Broadway theatre, through the worst bottleneck of traffic in the world, just to exchange smiles or tears with Miss Booth. Personally, I demand a little more. But if we want to know what theatre is, we should know what is "the least of it"—the minimum condition under which it can be said to exist.

What, by contrast, is the most that theatre could ever hope to offer? Or, at any rate, what is the most it ever *has* offered? To keep this essay within bounds I shall forget about dance, pantomime and song, and concentrate on the art which can advance the best claim to be the principal theatre art: the drama.

Histories of the drama customarily trace a development from what are called primitive beginnings to the great periods of flowering. But there is something misleading in the procedure, because, in the so-called primitive phases, art frequently shows what is called sophistication and, occasionally, far from remaining content with minimum demands, reaches out toward the maximum satisfaction. An instance is the art of tragedy at the moment of its very inception, as conjecturally established by Jane Harrison:

> . . . we are apt to forget that from the *epos,* the narrative, to the *drama,* the enactment, is a momentous step, one, so far as we know, not taken in Greece till after centuries of epic achievement, and then taken suddenly, almost in the dark, and irrevocably. All we really know of this momentous step is that it was taken some time in the sixth century b.c. and taken in connection with the worship of Diony-sos. Surely it is at least possible that the real impulse to the drama lay not wholly in "goat-songs" and "circular dancing places" but also in the cardinal, the essentially dra-matic, conviction of the religion of Dionysos, that the worshipper can not only worship, but can become, can *be,* his god.[3]

Perhaps this passage suggests too much. If some historians write of the later drama as if it were all but a falling away from Greek tragedy, Miss Har-

3. *Prolegomena to the Study of Greek Religion.*

rison likes to hint that even Greek tragedy might
be a falling away from that first sublime instant
when the worshiper of Dionysos became god. To
me, the value of her idea is that it sets a standard:
after this, for example, we know what to expect of
a tragic hero. Aristotle's dry, accurate statement
that a hero must be above life size takes on larger
significance. Our eyes are opened both to the god-
seeking and the blasphemy in tragic heroes from
Oedipus to Halvard Solness. And we sense how
painful has been the loss when playwrights eschew
this god-seeking and blasphemy because neither
they nor their culture believe in heroes.

The origins of comedy also call to mind the
highest claims that the drama can make for itself.
For, though the exact circumstances are even less
certain than those of the origins of tragedy, there is
some agreement that comedy derives from sheer
celebration of fertility—of what Bernard Shaw
called the Life Force, and what modern culture in
general blithely nails down in that most outrageous of its simplifications, the word Sex. If in
tragedy we feel that we can be god, in comedy our
identification is with the spring, the seeds, the
crops to come. A feeling of oneness with nature is
at the bottom of it, a profound and dedicated
acceptance of life, and of sexuality as central to
life—an acceptance just as sadly lacking in mod-

ern culture as genuine hero worship. No wonder our wiser men, from Carlyle to D. H. Lawrence, plead with us to try and recapture the ancient wisdom, the ancient ecstatic attachments!

Yet, though the very origins suggest what the maximum achievement of the drama might be, it remains (*pace* Miss Harrison) for history and culture and individual genius to furnish the proof: in the fullness of time comes such a tragedy as *Hamlet*, such a comedy as *Le Misanthrope*. What has been added to the moment of ecstatic identification with the god, the hour of the celebration of sexual energy? In a word, that which separates man from the beasts, and that which it was the glory of Greece to display to the world in all its dignity and power: intellect, mind, reason. *Le Misanthrope* is chiefly words. The old comic rhythms are at work but are given no direct corporeal expression. Comedy has been elevated into the realm of the spirit. And *Hamlet* is surely the first protagonist in world drama whom one would call an "intellectual." These are extreme cases. Yet the point is equally well illustrated by, say, *The Birds* and the *Oresteia*. Though Aristophanes' play wears its masquerade origin on its sleeve—for it was traditional to use animal disguises—just as surely as the plays of Molière and Shakespeare it represents the transformation of the drama by intellect. Doubtless there is no gain without some loss, and it is a pity that Aristophanes' birds and beasts retain no magic from any primeval past; the gain is that the art of drama is now something that the master spirits of the age can devote themselves to. And, though there are still people who see Aeschylus as barely emerging from the murk of superstition, the *Oresteia,* no less than the philosophy of Aristotle or Plato, is the very symbol of Hellas and its victories of mind over matter, law over lawlessness, civilization over barbarism.

Pericles referred to Greek recreations as "provision for the spirit," and it is worth stressing the spiritual and intellectual side, because in our time the other side is so grossly over-stressed, most of all by writers on theatre. But I am far from wishing simply to swing to the other extreme from those who represent the drama to be primitive. The achievement of all great drama is precisely the spanning of *both* sides of man's nature, the spiritual and the physical, the intellectual and the emotional.

However high in the air of the spirit the branches of the drama may rise, the tree still has its primitive roots, even if, as I said at the outset, our view of the primitive is a little arbitrary. The latest and most erudite study of *Twelfth Night*—by Leslie Hotson—shows that play to be a none too distant relative of fertility ritual. Deeply steeped in Christianity as he is, Shakespeare delights to celebrate in his comedies something that pagans as well as Christians have always delighted to celebrate: fruitful marriage. *As You Like It* culminates in a "wedlock hymn":

> Wedding is great Juno's crown
> > Oh, blessed bond of board and bed!
> 'Tis Hymen peoples every town,
> > High wedlock then to be honorèd.

A Midsummer Night's Dream ends with Oberon's promise that the wedding night of all three couples will have results:

> > To the best bridebed will we
> > Which by us shall blessèd be
> > And the issue there create
> > Ever shall be fortunate!

And *The Tempest* has a little wedding masque at its very center:

> Honor, riches, marriage blessing
> Long continuance and increasing,
> Hourly joys be still upon you!
> Juno sings her blessings on you.
> Earth's increase, foison plenty,
> Barns and garners never empty,
> Vines with clustering bunches growing,

Plants with goodly burden bowing,
Spring come to you at the farthest
In the very end of harvest!

One of Shakespeare's first comedies, *Love's Labor's Lost,* is about the futility of attempting to thwart nature by a life of celibacy, and it ends with two of the loveliest invocations of seasonal myth in literature, the winter and spring songs. In one of the last comedies, *A Winter's Tale,* seasonal myth is not merely invoked at the end, it is pervasive. Starting from the modest but clear hint of the title, the play says everything there is to say about winter and spring, taken both literally and figuratively; and the fourth act is Shakespeare's paean to springtime, to the fact of coming into this world, and hence to the process by which we come into it. Reaching for a hyperbole to indicate that he will not break faith, Florizel says that, if he does,

Let Nature crush the sides o'the earth together
And mar the seeds within!

In other words, the destruction of the seeds of life, the creation of infertility, is the ultimate horror.

If the comedies were written in celebration of fertility, the tragedies were written out of a sense of the horror of infertility or rather, one might say, but for the present-day associations of the word, of

contraception. The extent of Lady Macbeth's villainy is measured by the statement that—if worst
comes to worst—she would be prepared to murder
the baby at her breast (Act I, Scene vii, ll. 54–59) ;
and the farthest reach of her husband's wickedness
is not the murder of king or friend but of Macduff's little children. Commentators have been
puzzled by Macduff's first remark after the terrible
news has sunk in: "he has no children." Some have
not wanted to take the "he" as Macbeth at all;
others have wished to limit the sense to "he has no
children for me to take revenge on." But surely the
speech is one of those supremely dramatic utter-
ances that leap out of a situation, illogical yet
prompted by some higher logic, spreading meaning in several directions. The childlessness of Macbeth—with all its associations: sterility, futility,
unnaturalness, lack of posterity—that is the main
idea.

Like Florizel, Macbeth uses the figure of the
killing of the seeds to express the idea of ultimate
horror. Even if all Nature is in disorder, he asks
the witches (Act IV, Scene i) , answer me—and the
series of hyperboles in which he asks them culminates in:

> though the treasure
> Of nature's germens tumble all together
> Even till destruction sicken (ll. 58–60) .

The same image appears at the very climax of *King Lear:*

> And thou, all-shaking thunder,
> Smite flat the thick rotundity o' the world!
> Crack nature's molds, all germens spill at once
> That make ungrateful man! (Act III, Scene ii, ll. 6–9.)

King Lear is about "unnaturalness between the child and the parent." The relation between Lear and Goneril is the precise opposite of that between Prospero and Miranda. And so when the old man casts about in his battered brain for the most terrible thing he can say, it is this:

> Hear, Nature, hear, dear goddess, hear!
> Suspend thy purpose if thou didst intend
> To make this creature fruitful.
> Into her womb convey sterility.
> Dry up in her the organs of increase,
> And from her derogate body never spring
> A babe to honor her! (Act I, Scene iv, ll. 297–303.)

I dwell now on the primitive elements partly because scholars have indeed done justice to the non-primitive elements and partly to show that "primitive" elements may be subtle and profound. Those who present Shakespeare as the practical man of the theatre who wanted to make money by providing a few evenings of soft emotion and broad fun will get as little comfort from the primitive part of *King Lear* as from its sophisticated, theological and Christian part. This, *en passant:* the main point is that *King Lear* is both primitive and sophisticated, and that the power in Shakespeare that most compels our admiration is the synthetic power, the ability to span two such worlds as these. Of this man, our supreme playwright, we may say: he encountered no gap which he could not bridge.

Modern scholars have performed a service when they have demonstrated how, in *King Lear,* Shakespeare miraculously managed to present the whole "Elizabethan world picture," the universe around, human society on earth and individual man, center and model of the other two. It is a pity that after reading these modern accounts we sometimes have to wonder if Shakespeare also had a mind of his own. One may legitimately appeal back from purely scholarly interpretation to the judgment of the great humanistic critics, many of whom were not primarily scholars. It is the poet Dryden who reminds us that Shakespeare is not only to be commended for summing up the thought of his time: none was ever in livelier direct touch than he with life. "All the images of Nature," Dryden says, "were still present to him." And, just as he brought together the primitive and the sophisticated, he lived in the happy possession, not only of the world without, but of the world within. "He was the man who of all Modern, and perhaps Ancient Poets, had the largest and most comprehensive soul."

Having thrown out a hint or two as to what the drama was like in the beginning and what it became in the hands of its greatest practitioner, I turn to the modern stage. Necessarily, in this field, I shall be less concerned with attainments already completed than with problems reaching out into the future. But, first, what is to be inferred from the story I have been telling? Before asking what a new theatre can mean, should we not ask more searchingly what the old theatre means, what place it deserves in our lives? Shakespeare had such and such an intellect, such and such an imagination. To what end did he have them?

Some have said that the end of drama, and art in general, is pleasure, and others have said that it is instruction, and, though this is no place either to recapitulate or continue the argument, a remark or two about it may push the present enquiry one step further along. When, in her admirable book *Ancient Art and Ritual,* Jane Harrison chides those who see pleasure, not spiritual nourishment, as the end of art, is she not, like almost every contributor to this particular discussion, simply quibbling? Does she not find pleasure precisely in spiritual nourishment, just as we all do in non-spiritual nourishment? And, conversely, when Aristotle proposes pleasure as the end of art, does he not define pleasure so broadly as fully to appease those of Miss Harrison's persuasion, if they will read him sympathetically? One of the best commentators writes:

> . . . Aristotle recognizes specific differences between pleasures. There is the harmless pleasure, which is afforded by a recreation or a pastime: but a pastime is not an end in itself, it is the rest that fits the busy man for fresh exertion, and is of value as a means to further work; it has in it no element of that well-being or happiness which is the supreme end of life. . . . But art in its highest idea is one of the serious activities of the mind which constitute the final well-being of man. Its end is pleasure, but the pleasure peculiar to that state of rational enjoyment in which perfect repose is united with perfect energy.[4]

Such a form of pleasure is no less noble or moral than the objective proposed by those who take

4. S. H. Butcher: *Aristotle's Theory of Poetry and Fine Art.*

drama to be didactic—Shelley, for instance, who, in his preface to *The Cenci,* beautifully said:

> The highest moral purpose aimed at in the highest species of the drama is the teaching the human heart, through its sympathies and antipathies, the knowledge of itself.

I propose to accept all three viewpoints—Jane Harrison's, Aristotle's and Shelley's—and pass on to the problem of modern drama.

It could be that, in the eyes of the gods, there is no Problem of Modern Drama, no special and different task for the modern writer. Even so, we who are not gods can only see a perennial task in its urgent and present form. "Teaching the human heart the knowledge of itself," says Shelley. Assuredly he spoke for all time. Nevertheless, in the age following his death, the perennial task took a form which, it seems to me, can be roughly expressed in the words: teaching the human heart that it still exists. Or, better perhaps: teaching the human heart that it can exist again, that it can be brought back to life.

Ortega y Gasset says that man is the only creature who is made and not just born; for a man who simply exists is no man.

> What is a man
> If his chief good and market of his time
> Be but to sleep and feed?

Hamlet answers himself: "A beast, no more," and goes on to explain that this sleeping, feeding body of ours becomes human only when "godlike reason" inhabits it. Beasts are beasts, and gods are gods, but the human race is somewhere betwixt and between; that is the tragedy of our situation, and the comedy of it too. Now it may just be the way we feel about things, rather than an objective fact, but it does seem to us, does it not, that we live at a time when our humanity runs an unprecedented risk of total submersion in the beast? In such a time of death, the least flicker of life shines like a torch. In such a time of hate, the least murmur of love is music. In such a time of bestiality and unreason, the rediscovery of truly human impulse becomes the one thing necessary. And this is so far from being an original observation on my part that it is, on the contrary, the theme—one might almost say, the obsession—of modern literature, including dramatic literature. There is a line of Schiller that sums it up in advance:

Dass der Mensch zum Menschen werde
(That man may become man)

And this line is cited by Dmitri Karamazov in a crucial chapter that Dostoevsky calls "The Confession of a Passionate Heart in Verse." Or consider Browning's phrase, "and paint man man, whatever the issue." It is the second part of it that gives the modern application to the Shelleyan and perennial idea. "Whatever the issue!" There is a danger of man's being crowded out by "issues," a danger not just for people in general but particularly for the classes whose education should have made them champions of the human. We talk of "confusing the issue," but perhaps we should talk, rather, of issues that confuse us.

The aim, then, is the rediscovery of man, and one is tempted to say that the modern writer in the serious genres who ignores this aim is off the main track. Nor is it enough to be aware of the aim. The writer must be engaged in the process of search.

What is the difference between a novelist like Somerset Maugham and one like Joseph Conrad? In Aristotle's terms: Maugham offers us a pastime, Conrad the higher happiness which is the true end of human life. In more modern terms: Maugham is a proficient technician and entertainer, but Conrad is a searcher for the meaning that we too stand in need of, he is our companion and guide in the great quest.

The difference between Conrad and Eugene O'Neill is something else again. I believe that O'Neill wanted to achieve in the drama exactly what Conrad did achieve in the novel. If he didn't succeed, it could be simply that he had less talent, or it could be that, while he intended to search, he did not really do so. Reading *Mourning Becomes Electra,* we feel that here is an author who has said to himself: "What are tragedies like? They're about this, aren't they? They begin this way, proceed that way and end thus?" Reading *Lord Jim,* we join the author in a life-and-death struggle for meaning, for courage, dignity, identity, the humanly genuine, the human essence. And we forget how Conrad is doing it. Form is so perfectly handled that it disappears, and we confront the content in its nudity.

It is natural that, in approaching the topic of tragedy in modern times, we at once encounter Dostoevsky and Conrad.[5] There are no greater modern masters of tragedy than these, just as there are no greater modern masters of comedy than Jane Austen and Charles Dickens. Whatever justice there may be in saying that the drama has been dying, it would certainly be an error to imply that the energy that used to go into drama has petered out. At worst, it has been deflected into another channel, that of fiction, leaving the theatre a cultural backwater.

It would not be reasonable to show surprise, let

5. Anyone who considers this statement either pat or vague should read, among other things, Vyacheslav Ivanov's book on Dostoevsky, *Freedom and the Tragic Life,* especially the chapter entitled "The Novel-Tragedy."

alone indignation, that many plays are not very good; many novels are not very good either. What is disturbing is the extent to which theatre people are simply out of touch—with just about everything. And a corollary of this proposition is that our theatre writers do not address themselves to the common task. Their plays are all rehash. Drama has become a ragbag for yesterday's notions and fads. More depressing than the mere lack of achievement is the lack of ambition, of dedication, of the sense of what the drama has been and should be.

One does not ask that every novelist be a Conrad. One does ask, though, that every novel that is to be read right through to the end bear witness to its author's adventurous spirit. He must battle with the materials even if he doesn't always win. He must search even if he doesn't always find. He *must*—if only for technical reasons. For it is the act of searching that brings writing alive. Just barely alive, perhaps. Great writing is *more* alive than that, alive in more ways than that. But the searching mind can create a minimum of life. And this is a minimum that most playwrights today neither meet, nor try to meet nor have any idea they should try to meet. (Eugene O'Neill did not always meet it, but because he always tried to meet it, he is indeed a "distinguished" playwright; for

76

this fact distinguishes him from nearly all his colleagues.)

Two mistakes are made. First, playwriting is regarded simply as a craft. Now, clearly, playwriting *is* a craft, just as fiction is a craft, *among other things*. It is another question whether it is advisable to isolate the craft from those other things, thus in effect replacing the playwright with the play-doctor, which is rather like replacing fathers and mothers with midwives. The notion has spread among writers, play-doctors, critics, producers, actors, public, that plays are "not written, but re-written"; that is, not written, but pieced together, not composed with one man's passion and intellect but assembled by the ingenuity of all who stop by at the hotel bedroom, preferably during the rehearsal period. In this way, dramaturgy is demoted from the fine to the useful arts; and is unique among the latter by not really being useful.

The second mistake is to write with the audience consciously in mind, instead of in the faith that there will be an audience for good work. Obviously when we say that a play is not a writer's exploration of reality but just a calculated arrangement of effects, there is no need to ask: effects upon whom? The *raison d'être* of these effects is to interest and please the audience. All writers, of

77

course, *hope* to interest and please an audience; the exploratory writer decidedly hopes that his explorations will interest and please an audience. But for the non-exploratory writer, hope is not enough. He is not prepared to leave it, as it were, to chance. He puts his whole mind on audience, audience, audience—by God, he'll *make* them like it—and, perhaps, by foregoing his claim to be an artist, becomes a remarkable craftsman. An artist cannot give *all* his attention to the audience; he needs to keep so much of it for his characters, his story, his subject.[6]

Now I am not prepared to argue with anyone who merely expresses an arbitrary preference for craft and pastime over art and exploration. The argument starts when someone, like Walter Kerr in his book *How Not to Write a Play,* seeks to confer a higher status on the lower phenomenon, raising craft above art, or so defining art that, to all intents and purposes, it *is* craft. Perhaps Mr. Kerr would say he hasn't done this; and it is probably as hard for me to sum up a book of his in terms acceptable to him as it has certainly proved for him to sum up a book of mine in terms acceptable

6. In his book *The Inmost Leaf,* Alfred Kazin speaks of "that morbid overconsciousness of the audience that afflicts even the most serious writers in this country." The problem is one, not for the theatre alone, but for our culture generally.

to me. But I think it is true to say that he sees dramaturgy as a matter of adjusting the play to the audience; in no measure or fashion must the audience be asked to adjust itself to the play.[7] They pay their money and they take their choice. *Vox populi, vox dei,* with *populus* defined as non-intellectuals, shopgirls preferred.

What about intellectual shopgirls? That they exist is news that apparently hasn't reached Mr. Kerr, though it is familiar enough to any book publisher; and, of course, they stay away from the plays that Mr. Kerr tries so hard to enjoy on their account. I believe Mr. Kerr's invitation to shopgirls will be turned down because the intellectual ones are busy with paper-back books, while the non-intellectual ones are quite happy with their TV sets; for, if we want a truly popular alternative to such highbrow pursuits as reading, we have it—in TV. The theatre, as Mr. Kerr presents it, is something neither kind of shopgirl wants.[8] Nor is

7. Contrast this with the attitude of a great playwright: ". . . no matter how badly my *Carlos* fails as a stage-play, I must insist that our public could see it performed ten times more before it would comprehend and exhaust all the good in it which offsets its defects. . . ."—Friedrich Schiller.

8. "By current measurements of audience size, the theatre hardly qualifies as a means of mass communication. But the films assuredly do, and increasingly since the successful marketing of the paper-backs, so does the book."—J. Donald Adams, *The New York Times Book Review,* March 25, 1956.

79

his sociology so up-to-date as he would wish it to be. For example, the notice in the window of the five-and-ten-cent store at the end of my street in Manhattan does not read: SHOPGIRL WANTED. It reads: SALESLADY WANTED. Call it elegance, call it snobbery, the cold fact remains that no candidate who appeals to The Shopgirl Vote, from this time out, is going to get it.

Just as there is a word—patrioteering—for the kind of patriotism that is merely an appeal to the gallery or worse, there ought to be a word for that sort of "democratic" argument which is merely an appeal to mediocrity and the fear of distinction, for in America this is the appeal almost everyone makes when he runs out of real arguments: "democrateering," if I may coin a word and adjust a dictum, is the last refuge of a scoundrel. Mr. Kerr being no scoundrel, I shall dismiss his democrateering as simply unworthy of him, and turn to that part of his argument which calls for an answer. Discussing poetic drama, Mr. Kerr says: "Verse is of no value whatever unless, like every other part of the play, it mirrors the picture people have of themselves. . . . Writing verse is almost like taking the blood pressure of the age." If only Paddy Chayefsky would take up verse, one concludes, he would inevitably become Mr. Kerr's favorite playwright. For, even speaking prose, the actor who played Marty was awarded a golden urn with an inscription stating that he revealed "the meatcutters of America as friendly, humble, sincere, and accredited members of the human race." And this statement is guaranteed to give the picture the meatcutters have of themselves, as the urn was the gift of the Meatcutters Union, Local 587, Santa Monica, California. It seems to me that Mr. Chayefsky is the playwright of the age of conformity, the age of "other-directed" yes-men, the age of democrateering salesmanship; and that Mr. Kerr is in some danger of becoming its critic.

"Every . . . part of the play . . . mirrors the picture people have of themselves." As the metaphor was presumably suggested by a famous passage in *Hamlet,* it may not be unfair to ask what that passage means. Hamlet spoke of the actor as holding up the mirror not to the picture people have of themselves but to nature, that is to people as they really are—a very different matter. In his use of this figure, Shakespeare was following an established tradition according to which the mirror was held up to human affairs to the end that men might be inspired by a good example or warned by a bad one. It was a normative mirror. Though art imitated life, it did not do so just for the record, but in order to improve life; far from saying: "This is how you see yourself, humble, sincere and accredited; keep it that way," it said: "You see what happened to this bad king, go thou and do differently."

The derivation of Mr. Kerr's view is not from the older medieval and Renaissance tradition at all, but from that much more recent historicism which encourages us to see in literature the background, and not the writer—the "Elizabethan world picture," and not the great William Shakespeare. One of the few authorities cited for Mr. Kerr's highly debatable remarks on Shakespeare is an able journalist, Miss Marchette Chute. Admittedly, Miss Chute does not stand alone. She could easily appeal her case to a higher court, where such judges as Professor Alfred Harbage of Harvard and Professor Allardyce Nicoll of Birmingham sit on the bench. For out of a few false analogies with our situation today, and a great deal of rancor against the idea of minority culture, these and other celebrated scholars have created the image of a Shakespeare who would have given one hand to Mr. Chayefsky and the other to the selection committee of the Book-of-the-Month Club.

Without wishing to deny that Shakespeare was popular, I decline to forget that, equally, he was "unpopular," aristocratic; his being both at the same time, his belonging to *both* the popular culture *and* the court culture, being another aspect of his universality, his comprehensiveness of soul, and another reason why we must consider him supremely great. Therefore, since we are citing authorities, I should like to appeal over the heads of the Shakespeareans of the past generation to the Shakespeareans of many earlier generations, as, for example, to Thomas Carlyle who wrote: ". . . Shakespeare is . . . the greatest intellect who, in our recorded world, has left record of himself in the way of Literature." And, of course, it is not a matter of Shakespeare but of theatre, drama, and literature generally. I should like to oppose to this idea of a poet who merely takes the blood pressure of the age the idea of a poet who raises the blood pressure of the age.

Not that this will surprise Mr. Kerr, who suspects that what I want to do with the theatre audience is to make it suffer, give it heart failure, and kill it off, except for that tiny circle of sophisticates, highbrows, esthetes, longhairs and eggheads, up there in the top left-hand corner of the second balcony, who are the fellow-members of my mutual-admiration society. . . . In his book, Mr. Kerr rebukes a playwright who said he wished to make his audience uncomfortable. Now, of course, if the choice is simply between comfort and discomfort, pleasure and pain, we're all going to be on Mr. Kerr's side, including, I am sure, the playwright

G

who spoke of making his audience uncomfortable. Real life, however, mixes its pleasures and pains. Where is there more fun—in a comfortable play that gives auntie back her picture of auntie or an uncomfortable play which, while it may annoy auntie a bit, also intrigues her, tickles her, interests her, livens her up, and perhaps even shakes and moves her? [9] And in case anyone suspects that what I'm after is a little fun at auntie's expense, let me confess that sometimes I am auntie. Arthur Miller's plays pain me very much, but I would far rather see one of them than any play that, so to speak, merely reminds me of home, giving me back the pleasant picture I have of myself. Surely we do *not* want back our own image of ourselves. That way lies a dull and even degenerate sort of art. We want someone else's image, and not necessarily of themselves, but perhaps of someone else again. (For example, William Shakespeare's image, not of himself, but of Richard III.) By all means, there has to be established an identification of the audience with the action and, often, with a protag-

9. On the fact that people say of a show that is the rage, "You *must* go, but for my own part it bored me to death," William Archer commented: ". . . if the play is really a successful one, they misrepresent their sensations. . . . What they mean is, 'It interested me in spite of myself. I disliked it and it puzzled me; but it bored me much less than the trumpery pieces I like and understand.' "—*The Theatrical World of 1897.*

onist; but this is effected, not by bringing the protagonist to the audience, but, contrariwise, by
bringing the audience to the protagonist, lifting
them out of themselves, placing them in the skin of
a stranger.

> . . . the cardinal, the essentially dramatic
> conviction . . . that the worshipper can . . .
> become, can *be,* his god.

His god, says Jane Harrison; not himself; much
less his flattering image of himself. The tragic
hero, says Aristotle, is above life size; and comic
characters are below life size. Absolutely no one, in
the drama, is life size; no one is "the average shopgirl." Either our sense of reverence builds the hero
up, or our sense of scorn cuts the shopgirl down.
The theatre has a Brobdingnag and a Lilliput to
offer, but absolutely nowhere for the common man
to lay his head.

I am told that it is old-fashioned to speak of the
"commercial" theatre, for everyone now knows
that what Shakespeare and Shaw were after was
money. Another false trail! No one denies that, so
far from being against money, the artist is most
often in the position of having to say to the business man, as Shaw did to Samuel Goldwyn:
"You're only interested in art, I'm only interested
in money." Human beings like money, and an

artist is a human being. But he is also an artist, and while sometimes it may happen that the commercial theatre is mainly favorable to his art, it may sometimes happen that it is not—like the commercial anything else. Today, to choose a contrary example, commercial publishing in this country cannot, in my opinion, be said to be hostile to literature; on the contrary, any novel with merit in it has a strong chance of publication. In theatre, the situation happens to be very different. Not that there are great new plays lying idle in desk drawers; the trouble lies deeper than that. The plays don't get to be written at all, because those who might write them actually write novels. There are many answers to the question: what scares them off the theatre? One typical deterrent is the phenomenon of the Perfect Play.

The commercial play is the Swiss watch of dramaturgy. When properly manufactured, it is perfect, as only a piece of machinery can be perfect. And it is the prospect of such a perfection that current theatre criticism holds out to the young playwright, while enjoying itself noting the imperfections in plays by real writers. In this the newspaper critics live out their manifest destiny as spokesman of the status quo—or rather, like the Devil in *Don Juan in Hell,* not of the status quo as it actually is, but as it aspires to be, not of Broadway as it actually is, but of the Platonic idea of Broadway, not of what people are, but of the picture they have of themselves. The Perfect Play being a good deal easier to put together (though not easy) than a significant imperfect play, one can indeed conceive of a Broadway on which every play is perfect. And since the standard by which perfection is judged is clear and objective (namely, show of hands), all plays in which imperfections are found could be promptly removed from the boards and from the record. I think I have stumbled here on a suggestion that should earn me a medal—or an aisle seat at a perfect play—in whatever mechanized Utopia awaits us in the years to come.

Retreating to my customary persona, I realize that I am left with the unhappy task of championing imperfection. I idealize failure, says Mr. Kerr (to which it seems almost like nose-thumbing to retort: you worship success). Red herring upon red herring! It is not the price to be paid, but the jewel paid for, on which the case rests. But the price does have to be paid; the price of artistic success being, in general, a good deal of failure. To establish oneself as a VIP with a hit written at the age of twenty, and then to manufacture another hit every two years for life—this experience does not resemble that of any artist whose career is known to me. An artist begins as a fumbler, at best a brilliant fumbler, and, even after he has enjoyed some public success, he relapses continually into failures which no one should be so foolish as to idealize, since they represent to him nothing but bitterness and desolation of spirit. The lives of those two notorious career men, Shakespeare and Shaw, are not exceptions. Not even Shaw. The middlebrow critics of the Eighteen Nineties were all against the young highbrow who wrote *Arms and the Man;* he had no success then, and he had very little success with the plays of his last twenty-five years. When today *The Lark* is spoken of as "second only to *Saint Joan,*" it is well to remember which show came second as a Broadway run.[10]

(If those who champion pastime tend to be against art, those of us who are for art must make it crystal clear that we are not against pastime. There have grown-up particular pastimes, like Perfect Plays, which stand in the way of art, which in a sense are designed to replace art, but, no more than Aristotle when he formulated the distinction, need we in any way disapprove of pastime as such. On the contrary, we acquire in the theatre such

10. Namely, *Saint Joan,* with 218 performances (1923–24), as against *The Lark's* 229 (1955–56). Nor is it accurate to say that all runs were short in the Twenties. During the 1923–24 season there were seventeen plays on Broadway that had run for more than 500 performances, the greatest classics among them being *The Bat* and *Abie's Irish Rose.*

respect for certain lighter works and forms that we are ready to speak of the *art* in them, and so to pass beyond the dichotomy I have been using. The works of Labiche and Offenbach are pastimes. Are they therefore not art? The works of Dumas *fils* are not pastimes. Must we therefore rank them higher than Labiche and Offenbach? At this point, the terminology lets us down as, at some point, all critical terminology does. Before continuing to use the art-pastime dichotomy for what it is worth, I want, parenthetically, to concede this, and to insist that what I am trying to measure is the degree, not of earnestness, but of spiritual curiosity.)

I have been maintaining that the "serious" modern playwright is, or should be, engaged, along with other modern writers, in the search for the human essence. If it is possible to state in a word what moral quality the artist engaged in this quest needs above all others, I should say that it is audacity. Conversely, artists who are not searching, not reaching out for anything, but working comfortably within their established resources, and who are completely lacking in daring, who never "cock a snoot," "take a crack" at anything, "stick their necks out"—for them should be reserved the harshest adjective in the critical vocabulary: innocuous. In life there are worse things than innocuousness—forms of rampant evil which render innocuousness praiseworthy by comparison. But the Devil doesn't write plays. And when Mussolini wrote them he didn't succeed in projecting anything of the force of his iniquity. Like many a better man, he only succeeded in writing innocuously. But that is the worst type of writing there is.

With the two conceptions of work—art and pastime, exploration and craft—go two conceptions of the worker. The master of pastime is the well-adjusted person, happily holding hands with the audience.[11] The artist, if not maladjusted, and I believe he is not, is not well-adjusted either; perhaps we should follow Peter Viereck's suggestion and invent a third category, that of the *un*adjusted man, the healthy rebel. At any rate, it has been known, at least since Plato, that the artist is a dangerous character, and consequently that art is a subversive activity. I am not speaking of the philosophy, much less of the politics, of artists. Artists are disturbing, unsettling people, not by what they preach but by what they are, conservatives like Dante and Shakespeare being far more disturbing

11. "The secret of your theatrical prosperity," Scribe was told in the speech that welcomed him into the Academy, "is to have happily seized upon the spirit of your century and to have made the kind of play which it takes to most readily and which closely corresponds to its nature." Allowing for differences in vocabulary, isn't this what a Broadway critic would say when conferring an award on a Broadway playwright?

and unsettling than our little revolutionaries. The greater the artist, the greater the upset.

In the voice of every artist, however full-throated and mellow, there is an undertone of something very like insolence. The small boy who said to Mme. de Pompadour: "*Why* can't you kiss me? The queen kisses me," was not the devastating Voltaire but the "mild" Mozart. "To kindle art to the whitest heat, there must always be some fanaticism behind it": Bernard Shaw was inspired to write this by seeing, not Ibsen's *Ghosts,* but the music-hall sketches and cabaret songs of Yvette Guilbert. The famous Tramp of Charlie Chaplin was gentle, and beloved by all the world, yet when I heard a candid spectator say of Charlie: "I can't stand the man," I realized how many others would say the same if they rigorously examined their responses; because, for all the charm and the high spirits, Chaplin is an alarming artist. Again, I am not referring to politics (though doubtless Chaplin took up Stalinism because he *thought* it was radical; there, history's joke was on Charlie). About any film of his, however slight, there is an air of menace; whereas most other comedians, for all that they make a lot more noise, are quite harmless.

Henri de Montherlant devoted an essay to the analogy of playwriting and bullfighting; and I have heard Martha Graham compare the dancer to the matador, and that, not in point of similarity of movement, but similarity of psychology: the dancer will attain to that razor-edge keenness when each move, each fall, each leap has that degree of urgency, that heightened sense of hazard.

"Live dangerously!" The artist follows Nietzsche's recommendation. Ortega y Gasset says there is some vulgarity in it because life is of its nature dangerous. True; but, as the fact is ignored and implicitly denied by modern culture as such, Nietzsche was fully justified in shouting it from the housetops. Even now, though editorials can be uselessly shrill about hydrogen bombs, though facts like the murder of 6,000,000 Jews are common knowledge, that fundamental complacency of middle-class culture—the most imperturbable of all imperturbabilities—is still with us. The works of Nietzsche have not "dated." Nor has the artist's sense of danger: precisely from his "subversiveness" stems his utility to society.

And the theatre could make a special contribution. For though it has sometimes chosen to be the most unenterprising of the arts, the genius, and even the very technics, of the medium tend all the other way. Theatricality is, *by definition*, audacious. A comedian is, *by definition*, a zany. The impertinence, insolence, effrontery that I have spec-

ulatively attributed to the artist in general none
would deny to the clown in particular. But have
we begun to draw the logical inferences? We have
been told often enough of all the gradual, thor-
ough and fine-spun things that the novel can do
and that the stage fails to do, but have we explored
the possibilities of theatre in the opposite direction—the realm of the sudden, the astonishing, the
extravagant? The theatre is the place for the anarchist to throw his bomb.

Or perhaps for anyone *but* the anarchist to
throw his bomb. For while theatre is the art of
explosions, the trick is to have them go off at the
right time in the right spot. Audacity has no place
in the arts until it is brought under iron control.
The rhythm of theatre derives from an alternation
of explosion and silence; more precisely, there is
preparation, explosion and subsiding. The man of
the theatre must not merely bring explosives in his
bag; he must know exactly how to prepare the
explosions and how to handle their subsidence.
For the interplay between audacity and control
produces the supreme artistic effects; the work of
the masters of dramatic literature abounds in examples. And stage directing calls for the same com-
bination of powers, though usually, even from the
expert, we get either audacity without control, or
control without audacity. The only man I know of

who is endowed with both gifts to the greatest possible extent—and in both fields, playwriting and directing—is Bertolt Brecht. In that fact—and not in the theory and practice of propaganda—lies the secret of his unique importance in the theatre today.

But I am not coming forward with a messiah. No one man will provide the answer to our problem, and to part of it Brecht provides, in my opinion, the wrong answer. He is one of those writers who search less and less after what I have been calling the human essence, because they are more and more convinced that they have already found it. Even supposing that Brecht *has* found it, that fact would not augur well for him as an artist. The only artists today who remain artists after conversion to causes which claim a monopoly of the truth are those who are not wholly convinced. Graham Greene's work derives its vitality now from the fact that he is always fighting his own Catholicism. The minute he says to himself, "I am a Catholic writer," begins to ask the alleged truth of his beliefs to do duty for his personal grasp of truth, however tentative and unsure, he is through. I am not objecting here either to Communism or Catholicism but, rather, pointing out what kind of adherence to these causes, or any other that makes comparable claims for itself, is damaging to an artist. The audacity for which I have praised Brecht was not the product of such an adherence but, on the contrary, of that bourgeois freedom in which Brecht gradually came to disbelieve. As he was an artist by virtue of his subversive activities, and socially and overtly subversive activities at that, absolutely necessary to his art was a society which, first, he wished to subvert and which, second, would permit him to try and subvert it. Bourgeois capitalism met both conditions; Soviet communism neither. And so the *enfant terrible* of the Weimar Republic tried to convert himself into the yes-man of the Soviet bureaucracy and the DDR (Deutsche Demokratische Republik). Only in relation to the West could this political writer even try to remain audacious, and this is that easy audacity (common also among anti-Communists) which is no audacity at all.[12] Meanwhile, those larger works which Brecht hopes will have some lasting value are most alive where some unresolved inner conflict forces its way in despite the author and the watching bureaucrats. Into both *Galileo* and *Mother Cour-*

12. My comments on Tennessee Williams and Arthur Miller in my books *What is Theatre?* and *The Dramatic Event* are an attempt to describe the phenomenon of easy, or false, audacity in current American drama. This is not to deny that both these authors are capable of real audacity; their superiority to most of their colleagues derives to a large extent from such greater daring.

age have been smuggled elements which are as subversive to Communism * as *The Threepenny Opera* is to capitalism. The Communist press has not been entirely happy about either play.

It is a mistake even to hope that an ideal will find its realization in a single man. It is a mistake to expect that the ideal situation will ever be realized at all. And it is above all a mistake to think that ages of great theatre come about through the critics' explaining how to write plays, or even how not to write them. The critic's influence is not directly on the creative act but on public opinion (the playwright being, however, a member of the public) . What the critic influences is morale.

The theatre today is demoralized. It suffers from hysterical oscillation between cheap cynicism and idealistic euphoria. This could be because dramatic art nowadays attracts chiefly manic depressives, though to say so only provokes the query: how has this come to be so? Between flat despair and yeasty zeal, why is there nothing but a vacuum? The question puts the cart before the horse: it is precisely because of this vacuum, this void,

---

* Again it is necessary to note that, at the date of writing, "Communism" meant "Stalinism." Secondly, some posthumous works of Brecht show him as less of a yes-man than is stated in this essay, written before Brecht's death. As for the insufficiency of my own formula, see "The Theatre of Commitment" below.

this *néant,* that men can only admit defeat or simulate success, descend to cynicism or rise to feverish and showy enthusiasm. Which is to repeat that they are demoralized.

Now, if it isn't too late, what do we do about demoralization in any institution—the church, the army, the nation—but try to recall people to a sense of the past, the glorious origin of the institution, its great men, its highest moments? And this is what I have been doing in the course of this brief attempt to answer the question: What Is Theatre? (or rather, this lengthy attempt to ask that question). We of the theatre need the inspiration and the discipline of Shakespeare and Molière exactly as a musician needs the inspiration and discipline of Bach and Mozart. And we need a sense of where it all came from, this theatre of ours, and where it has been going, and where it seems to be going now. For the task that inexorably confronts us—the task of continuing—we need, also, to assign ourselves a master objective. I have been suggesting that it is to search for our lost humanity. And, as weapons in this quest, I have been commending two that have been there from the beginning without losing any of their efficacity with the passage of time—the audacity of Dionysos and the controlling hand of Apollo.

(1955–56)

97

TAKING IBSEN
PERSONALLY

AN ADDRESS GIVEN AT THE
UNIVERSITY OF OSLO
IBSEN WEEK, 1956

IBSEN'S INSTRUMENT was the Norwegian language. That is your instrument too; but not mine; so I come before you this morning, an amateur addressing professionals. And the position of the amateur has some advantages, albeit chiefly those of the fool rushing in where angels fear to tread.

In self-defense, I am going to invite you to remember that Ibsen was a *European* writer, by which I mean a writer known to the whole Western World—known, therefore, in all the languages of the Western World. Very few playwrights, even among the greatest, are European in this sense. Calderon, Racine and Schiller, for example, are totally absent from the English-speaking theatre and almost totally unknown to readers of English.

It was the special achievement of Ibsen and Strindberg—and Ibsen more than Strindberg—to con-
quer the foreigner. And so, if your critics blame us
foreigners for our blindness to the Norwegian
character of Ibsen's work, you should blame Ibsen
himself for being so cosmopolitan that he appealed
to us in the first place. To you, the action of *A
Doll's House* takes place, crucially and unmistakably, in Norway. Bernard Shaw, however, said it
took place in every suburb in Europe; and that,
despite the notorious imperfections of Ibsen trans-
lations, is how it seems to all of us non-
Scandinavians. Just as the Germans came to speak
of *Unser Shakespeare*, there is no non-Scandinavian
country that did not come to think of *its* Ibsen.

All this by way of excusing the announced title
of this address: What Ibsen Has Meant To Me,
which has an egoistic ring. I hope the curse of
egoism can be lifted from my observations this
morning by the typicality of the experiences reported. It isn't what Ibsen has meant to me alone
that I have in mind, but what he has meant to
non-Scandinavians in general. Yet Ibsen taught us
not to fear speaking for ourselves, for that way lies
the danger of speaking, not for everyone, but for
no one. I choose a personal approach in order, not
to be more exquisite or eccentric, but to be more
truthful.

When I was about fifteen, one of our teachers came to class and told us about a play that he'd just seen in London. He couldn't remember the names of the characters but he would call the leading one Sybil Thorndike because this actress played it. The plot was absolutely terrific—I think that was the way he put it—and the play ended with Sybil Thorndike's son going mad on stage, with poor Sybil Thorndike unable to make up her mind whether or not to keep her promise—which was to give him poison.

At a slightly later date, I came upon a copy of the play *Ghosts,* by Henrik Ibsen, in a small branch library of the Lancashire town where I grew up. Looking at the last page, I recognized my teacher's play. (A preface said something about an Italian actress who had evidently played Sybil Thorndike; the name was spelled DUSE, and I wondered how you pronounced it.) Reading the play through, I found the schoolmaster had exaggerated neither the circumstances of the story nor their effectiveness. I, too, found the play "absolutely terrific." The colloquial hyperbole seems, indeed, appropriate to the youthful enthusiasm I felt for an author who could stir me so deeply. I don't recall being so surprised by a book—caught off guard, as it were, completely "bowled over"—until, in college days, I read *Crime and*

Punishment. Or until, also during my college years, I first saw Ibsen staged.

It was *The Master Builder* in London with D. A. Clarke-Smith as Solness and Lydia Lopokova as Hilda Wangel. I had not read the play, and, again, I was surprised. And, after all, at every moment, what a surprising play this is! Where are we? Who *are* these people? And what on earth is going on? This is distinctly old-fashioned theatre, is it not, in which, when a character says the younger generation is knocking at the door, a knock is actually heard at the door, and in walks the ingénue? Yet why is that knock so strangely startling? One jumped in one's seat. The story is not very clear, is it, or at least not very comprehensible? What is all this that happened so long before the curtain went up? Are we meant to believe it all? That Solness shook his fist at God from the top of a tower? And did he really make this girl the promise she speaks of? And is it credible that she would come to him after all these years and expect him to keep such a promise? No, obviously not. And yet—and yet—if the fable is so unclear and incredible, how does it happen that we find ourselves caught in it? And caught we are—at any rate, caught I was. And I could not believe that the web I was caught in was merely the web of adroit dramaturgy as, say, with Scribe. There was something altogether more Sophoclean about it. It seemed the web of fate. Not that I found the *idea* of fate in it—rather, the *sense* of it, the sense of inevitability and grand significance. Somewhere, behind the middle-class prose of the dialogue, a great bronze gong was sounding. I have in mind, not subtlety of meaning, but the power of the effect. The *impact* and *enthrallment* that publishers like to claim for any new work they print are actually rarities. But even those who rate Ibsen lowest should grant that, in the theatre, enthrallment is something he can establish in the first seconds of the action and sustain unbroken throughout an evening, while the impact of the work as a whole is seldom short of shocking.

And so it happens that the Ibsen evenings stand out so strongly in my recollection of nearly a quarter century of theatre-going. Though much is forgotten, the special quality of each production remains, even when it is only one of Ibsen's special qualities shining through bad acting and inept direction. Among the best productions I have seen is that of *Ghosts* as presented by the Old Vic just before the Second World War with Marie Ney as Mrs. Alving and Emlyn Williams as Oswald. Though long stretches of the performance have faded from memory, certain moments have stayed quite luminously with me. And this is not as unsatisfactory a state of affairs as it sounds, for, while the atmosphere is charged from the beginning to the end of an Ibsen play, it is at a limited number of moments that the charge explodes, sometimes in thunder and lightning, sometimes in the characteristically Ibsenian lightning without thunder. It was a thunderous moment, in that production, when the sanatorium caught fire, and the thunder had a mocking sound when Manders cried out in pain because the place wasn't insured. Lightning flashed without thunder in the quietness of Emlyn Williams' first entrance (when Oswald confronts Manders with his anti-type), and in the hush of horror as Mrs. Alving hears the ambiguous noises from Oswald and Regina in the next room and realizes what they mean. (Miss Ney dropped a crumpled piece of paper, and one could hear it hit the floor.)

It would be easy to list the merits of other outstanding Ibsen performances I have seen—such as Michael Benthall's production of *The Wild Duck,* in which Anton Walbrook shuttled between the pathetic and the ridiculous with dazzling virtuosity—yet the point about Ibsen can perhaps be even better clinched by reference to a couple of performances that were not outstanding. A production of *Rosmersholm* at the Yale Drama School demonstrated to my satisfaction—and perhaps to my surprise—that even moderately good amateur performance, if conscientious and sensibly directed, can enthrall an audience and have a shocking impact—in short, create in the theatre the Ibsen magic, the Ibsen world.

My last exhibit is that of the worst Ibsen production I have seen: *The Master Builder* as produced a couple of years ago at the Phoenix Theatre in New York with Oscar Homolka as Solness and Joan Tetzel as Hilda Wangel. A resolute attempt was made to eliminate the poetry, the mythic quality, the suggestion of great gongs sounding, and reduce the play to the cliché romance of a tired businessman and the spirited young lady he prefers to his weary and wearisome wife. That the attempt failed shows Ibsen's play to be actor-proof. The great effects were indeed weakened, but they were not eliminated. For all the pretence of putting Ibsen on firm naturalistic ground, the tremor of the Ibsenian earthquake was still occasionally felt.

2

I have been trying to say what it is in Ibsen that first takes hold of us, and I shall now try to say what it is in him that *keeps* hold of us. What would explain, in my own case, my starting with Ibsen in a first book on modern drama and my ending with him years later in a book on modern theatre? Or, to give the question a more academic form, what is his abiding relevance now that, in the mid-twentieth century, all the initial shock of Ibsenism has long been absorbed?

The world's attitude to Ibsen has gone through two phases and is now, as I see it, entering upon a third. The first phase was that of the late nineteenth century, at which time one either expressed one's detestation of the dramatist's iconoclasm or one's enthusiastic acceptance of it. Either way, the Ibsen under consideration was the revolutionary; and one accepted or rejected him according to whether one was oneself a revolutionary or not.

The second phase of opinion came with the acceptance of Ibsen in the early twentieth century by society at large. A gain of this sort is always, at the same time, a loss. For general acceptance implies only a cessation of hostilities, not an active interest in an author. To be accepted is the first step toward being ignored. When the rear guard accepts an author, moreover, the advance guard drops him. Necessarily so, as the advance guard's function had been to scold the rear guard for underestimating him. Not so necessary, but quite natural, is the advance guard's tendency to turn against those it used to champion, perhaps even reviving arguments against them that had first been formulated by the rear guard. In the nineteenth century, playwrights were warned against Ibsen by the diehard, older critics; in the twentieth century they began to be warned against him by the advanced young spirits. Bertolt Brecht's Epic Theatre, beginning in the nineteen twenties, was, on the technical side, mainly a revolt against Ibsen, whose forms Brecht has described as rigid and narrow.

More important than the technical side, perhaps, was the ideological. As the only fully worked-out Marxist theory of drama, Brecht's Epic Theatre is the purest example of collectivism in twentieth-century dramatic writing, and the extreme statement of his thought is to be found in the play *Die Massnahme* (*The Measures Taken*), which celebrates the sacrifice of the individual to the group. Ruth Fischer credibly states that it is based on the experiences of her brother Gerhard Eisler as a Communist agent in China, and, by anticipation, it dramatizes the deaths of Radek and Bukharin, Rajk and Slansky, though not the subsequent admission, in 1956, that the confessions these men made were a pack of lies.

During the phase of history that produced Epic Theatre, collectivistic thought spread far beyond the confines of the Communist movement, and when I was in college in the nineteen thirties, the standard opinion was that Henrik Ibsen was *borné* and *petit bourgeois*—that he represented the end of individualism and not the beginning of the great new order. Only later did I learn that this view had first been expressed by Friedrich Engels himself and thereafter had been echoed by all Marxist critics from Mehring on.

And Marx and Engels were right, if their philosophy as a whole was right; it is a matter of that; while, equally, Ibsen will cease to seem *borné* and *petit bourgeois*, will become important again, to those who wish to stand *for* the individual and *against* what seems to them the hideous monolith of Soviet collectivism. To these—and you will realize that I am one of them—the great individualists of the nineteenth century are still great, Ibsen among them. Great and exemplary—for they possess what we have lost but must at all costs rediscover.

They possessed, first and foremost, what Lionel Trilling and others have been calling the mystique of the self: for their self-respect, and their belief in self-respect, went beyond opinion to sentiment, and beyond sentiment to faith. For them, there existed no Radeks and Bukharins—no people, that is, who could be asked to lie their lives away for an alleged collective good. In some much-quoted lines of verse, Henrik Ibsen once said that to live was to fight with the devils that infest the head and heart and to hold a Last Judgment over the self. The mystique of the self never found more pithy expression, nor the subject matter of Ibsen's plays more precise definition. Even where Ibsen criticizes an individualist—as in *Brand* and *The Wild Duck*—he does so, not from any standpoint acceptable to Marxism, but from that of another individualism. Brand's flaw, after all, is a defect in self-knowledge. Instead of living in harmony with his own nature, he attempts to live according to an abstract law which he must constantly foist on himself and others by arbitrary violence. This individualist becomes less of an individual all the time. By a supposed attachment to the *super*human, he becomes *in*human.

Consider Mrs. Alving, the individualist as woman. We know she reads the right books, though Ibsen leaves them unnamed so that each spectator can supply the titles of his own favorites. She belongs to the nineteenth-century Enlightenment. But we find out that she achieves enlightenment in general while keeping herself ignorant in particular of precisely those two or three things which it would do her most good to know: above all, of her complicity in the tragedy of Captain Alving. When she tells Oswald—at the end—that she shared the blame, because, in her prudishness, her fear of sexuality, she had not welcomed Alving's joy of life, she is also telling herself. Catastrophe in this story plays, as it were, the role of psychoanalysis, bringing to consciousness the guilty facts which the protagonist has so zealously kept under. Mrs. Alving, reader of books, has come to know many things; but she has not come to know herself. She is not too much an individual, as Manders thinks, but too little.

My generation of undergraduates—that of the nineteen thirties—reserved its greatest contempt for the person who was "only interested in saving his soul" and was therefore neglecting the real task, that of changing the world. We didn't realize to what an appalling extent the motive force of our reforming zeal was the fear of the self, the failure to face the self. We scoffed at the escapism of certain individualistic poets, and did not see that social collectivism could be the supreme escape, and conversely that there can be no healthy altruism which is not founded in self-respect. Yet, if we hadn't been tipped off that Ibsen was *petit bourgeois*, we might have learned our lesson from him. For he saw that the enlightenment in a Mrs. Alving was but the skin over the sore. He saw that the altruism of a Gregers Werle was the outgrowth of a sick conscience; Gregers persecutes Hedwig because he is running away from himself.

With the disrespect for the self that has been so prevalent in our time goes, naturally, a disrespect for the whole inner life of man, as witness the overtone that the word "subjective" now carries. The "objective" is real, the "subjective" is unreal—in other words, you get at the truth by getting away from yourself. If anyone remarked of Neville Chamberlain in 1938 that at least his motives were good, there was always a young Marxist on hand to remark that we must not judge by motives but by objective facts. Here again, Ibsen belongs to the earlier tradition. He believes the motive itself to be an objective fact and, in a strict sense, the primary fact—the one to start from. He would never have written a play about the rightness or wrongness of Chamberlain's policy, but he might well have written one about whether the man did indeed have good motives, whether his conscience was healthy. His plays are studies in *un*healthy conscience, in lack of integrity. Naturally, then, he seems not only old-fashioned but even wrongheaded to those who assume that life begins after integrity has been surrendered to a party, a class or a state.

But I do not wish to focus my whole argument upon Communism, because, in the present connection, Communism is only the extreme instance of a universal phenomenon—conformism parading as virtue. And in the West we encounter the danger less in the form of Communism than as a new attitude to life which the American sociologist David Riesman calls other-directedness—that is, being oriented toward other people, not just in external matters, not just, as it were, when other people are looking, but even in one's most intimate mental activity. Modern civilization lives under the sign of Mrs. Grundy.

The spiky, individualistic Victorians were, of course, inner-directed. Trained under strong fathers in the discipline of self-reliance, they hearkened to the inner voice, and went their independent way. Whether we can ever get back to anything of the sort is a question going far beyond the scope of the present statement. But even Mr. Riesman (who seems to be a fatalist) permits himself some unmistakably nostalgic admiration. And, certainly, the stock of all the Victorian individualists has been rising as men have come to realize what a frightful mess the anti-individualists have been making of the world. Ibsen is a great exemplar of the inner-directed culture. *Peer Gynt,* though not quite a prophecy of other-directedness, is about the danger of self-disrespect, of having no sense of identity, of being a human onion, all layers and no center.

III

By this time, I may have given the impression that What Ibsen Means To Me is Conservatism, the Nineteenth Century Darby and Joan, or even Songs My Mother Taught Me. Certainly we have come to the point where Victorianism no longer suggests a narrow and enervating stuffiness but manliness, free intellect, abundant individuality —men like Henrik Ibsen rather than Parson Manders. Of course, the great Victorians were *not* conservatives but rebels against Victorian-*ism,* non-conformists one and all. In political theory, Henrik Ibsen leaned toward anarch-ism—of all *isms* the most remote from totalitarian-ism. His first audiences regarded him as primarily a rebel, and in the future, I think, he will be regarded as a rebel again.

Ibsen's plays are *about* rebels— from Catiline to Brand and Julian, and from Lona Hessel and Nora Helmer to Hedda Gabler and John Gabriel Borkman. And we should not need to be told by Ibsen himself (as we were) that he wrote only of what he had lived through, for rebelliousness is very evidently not only the subject of the plays but the motive force. Anti-clericalism (as in the por-trait of Manders and the Dean in *Brand*) and political satire (as in *The League of Youth* or the characterization of the Mayor in *Brand*) are merely the most obtrusive signs of a mentality that was critical through and through. As we retreat in horror, disgust or mere boredom from the idea of the writer as Commissar or Official Mouthpiece, we come back to the old liberal conception, most adequately represented in this century by André Gide: the writer as questioner, dissenter, challenger, troublemaker, at war with his age, yet, by that token, standing for the best in his age and helping the age to understand itself. In Ibsen, as in Gide, we who live in a time of fake radicalism are confronted by a real radical.

In speaking of fake radicalism, I again have more than Communism in mind—more even than politics. I am thinking, for example, of all playwrights who are considered daring, and whose courage is rather lightheartedly connected by critics with that of Ibsen and Strindberg. As people these playwrights are often much more Bohemian than Ibsen. In fact, he seems distinctly prim by comparison. And, similarly, something much more quickly identifiable as daring is smeared over the whole surface of their plays, which deal with assorted neuroses not even mentionable in the theatre of Ibsen's day. But Ibsen is supposed to have given daring its start in *Ghosts*. . . .

The mistake here is to imagine that the subject of *Ghosts* is syphilis. Lucky for Ibsen that it isn't, as the medical science of the play is now quite obsolete! His daring was not a matter of bringing up repellent subjects, though it included that. It consisted simply in his genuinely radical attitude to life in general, and it is therefore at the heart of his writing and not merely on its surface.

What is true in the sexual sphere applies also to the political. In our political plays today, we are given what is conventionally regarded as daring but what actually takes no courage at all to say—it is at best what used to be daring and is now calculated to produce cheers from a clique, class or party rather than bad reviews in the press and rotten eggs from the gallery. An instance, oddly enough, is *An Enemy of the People* as freely adapted to the American stage in the mid-twentieth century by Arthur Miller. Ibsen's original, by contrast, though no profound piece of thought, and in my view one of his least vital plays, is genuinely daring, especially in its blunt challenge to the idea of majority rule. The reason the Miller version is dull is that Mr. Miller was himself offended by Ibsen's daring, made excuses for him in a preface, and proceeded to censor offensive passages. The dangerous thoughts of the latter-day quasi-radical are all completely safe; Ibsen's plays were so subversive they frightened, at times, even their author.

Another difference between the old radical and the new is that the former explored life while the latter lays down the law about it. *Die Massnahme* perfectly represents the latter procedure. Such a play is not even drama of discussion or ideas, for the author isn't talking it over with you, he is telling you. Still less is it drama of exploration, for the "play" is but a device to clinch the point the author started out with.*

Gerhart Hauptmann once remarked that the playwright must never re-word thoughts which he or his character has already thought: dramatic dialogue must only present thoughts in the process of being thought. Which is another way of saying that the playwright must not be directly didactic, for it is the didactic writer—out, not to learn, but to teach—who concentrates on finding effective form for thinking that was finished long ago. Didacticism seems not to have been a besetting temptation for Ibsen as it is for Brecht. It is an irony that the man who is always considered the father of the drama of ideas makes so few explicit references to ideas in his plays.

Incidentally, I consider *An Enemy of the People* inferior Ibsen just because it is one of the few plays in which this author seems simply to be "telling us"—with upraised finger and an inclination to be

---

* This breezy summary of Brecht's play passes over the not-so-secret sympathy shown for the Young Comrade. Brecht was not a monolith and neither, it was soon to turn out, was the world communist movement.

very angry if we aren't good and do as we're "told." Generally, with Ibsen, we feel we are his companions in a search and therefore, in line with Hauptmann's principle, are not given summaries of what has been thought already but are present at the thinking. Mere summaries of experience (intellectual experience or otherwise) are without dramatic life. The pulse of the drama begins to beat at the moment the playwright begins to struggle with his experience. There is indeed no better evidence for this truth than the life-work of Henrik Ibsen.

Hauptmann's principle enables us to understand the radical difference not only between Ibsen and Brecht but between Ibsen and the Ibsenites. The more the latter agreed with the Master, the worse the result was bound to be: for they were starting where he ended—namely, with his findings. It is of course open to writers who do this to improve on their master in all the external qualities of literature—elegance, concision, clarity and so on. For they are only paraphrasing. And it makes one realize that one values literature, ultimately, for other qualities than these. One will indeed suffer inelegance, inconcision, unclarity and the rest with a good grace if only there is a degree of inner movement, action, energy, conflict. . . .

There is a lesson in Ibsen for our so-called profession of playwrights today. The profession—by definition, perhaps—acquires a certain craft and then . . . uses it. In other words, the professional writer works within the resources he has found himself to possess. Such-and-such worked very well last time; the presumption that it may work well again is enough to prompt a second use, and a third and so on. Hence his youth is the professional writer's only creative period; there can indeed, on the terms just stated, be no development, but only a possibly increasing facility. Ibsen chose the path of constant development, accepting the risks, paying the price and reaping the reward. The price is the foregoing of easy success and small perfection. Professional dramatic critics, out of something more than fellow feeling, will always tend to prefer the professional craftsman to the real artist: the merits of what the former has to offer are more easily recognized and measured, while the latter undoubtedly makes far more mistakes, and is not always improving. The pay-off comes at the end, when the "mistake"—about which the critics have "rightly" been merciless—reveals itself as a needed part of a pattern. It has been said that all Shakespeare's plays taken together form one long play. Something of the kind can be said of the collected work of any real artist.

Not the smallest fascination of Ibsen is the togeth-
erness of his work, the profound meaning in the
relation of play to play. To write both *Brand* and
Peer Gynt is not just twice the job of writing one
of the two; it is to force the reader to read the plays
as thesis and antithesis in an artist's effort at syn-
thesis. To follow up *Ghosts* with *An Enemy of the
People* was more than an act of moral reprisal, and
to follow up *An Enemy* with *The Wild Duck* was
more than an act of self-correction: one thing leads
to another in a drama which has *Catiline* for pro-
logue and *When We Dead Awaken* for epilogue,
the drama of Ibsen's whole *oeuvre*.

Henrik Ibsen meant a lot to me when I first
encountered theatre, literature and adult life, and
I return to him a couple of decades later when
trying, as we do, to come to terms with the theatre,
the literature and the life around us, trying to
locate the essential problems, discard impeding
prejudices, correct obstructive errors, see through
the facts to the meaning of the facts—and, in all
this, to accept the self that does the locating, dis-
carding, correcting and seeing. For, while the
Bible tells us to love our neighbor as ourselves,
Henrik Ibsen seems to remind us how foolish that
injunction would be for people who do *not* love
themselves.

(1956)

THE PRO AND CON
OF POLITICAL
THEATRE

CON

ONE'S THINKING on this subject begins with the assumption that all the arts have a certain social importance. But do most members of most societies make this assumption? Probably not. So that, at the outset, the thinker finds himself in conflict with the world, and that is why what he says will be polemic rather than philosophy. But perhaps most thinking is polemical.

However this may be, it is certain that one is forced into a defensive posture. One is the champion of art against the philistines. And so it comes about that, in a world that doesn't believe in art at all, art is nearly always represented, in print, as having far more importance than it really possesses. A few great artists—Plato, for instance, and Tol-

stoy—have refused to swell the chorus of art wor-
shipers, but every sophomore learns to dismiss their
opinions on the point without for one moment
entertaining the possibility that they should have
been given a hearing.

If Plato and Tolstoy were mistaken, they are
mistaken in the same way as most of their critics:
they over-estimated the influence of art. If the artist
is not as dangerous as they thought, it is because
his work doesn't have that much effect one way or
another. I am speaking of tangible and overt influence—social influence. Didn't "good" works like
Uncle Tom's Cabin have much less effect on history
than Tolstoy thought? Isn't the same true of works
he deplored, such as his own masterpieces?

Not that these questions are dead simple. The
violent emotions that many experienced when
reading Mrs. Stowe are certainly "effects." What I
am questioning is whether such emotions played a
decisive, or even a large, part in the freeing of the
slaves. And if one followed up that discussion, one
would have to ask to what extent these good emotions are truly good. The emancipation was itself
highly ambiguous, and if Mrs. Stowe had influence
at all, we should also reckon with the way in which
she antagonized the enemy and helped to create
the present-day Southern intransigence. If her book
is useful today, it is useful chiefly, say, to a Governor

Faubus, who might justly cite it as an instance of Northern incomprehension.

At that, I will stand by the position that literature is much less important, in the worldly sense, than it has usually been assumed to be. Governor Faubus can get along very nicely without Mrs. Stowe. Don't be misled by the fact that literature can *seem* to have a political importance much larger than it actually commands. Boris Pasternak, for instance, has truly become important politically, but that is not to say that his writings have political influence. For one thing, they are profoundly unpolitical writings, but what I have in mind is, rather, that the name Pasternak does not stand, in the eyes of the millions who know of him, as the author of words they have read, but as the author of words they have read *about*. America is full of people who wept when they read in the paper of Pasternak's fate but who snored when they got to page ten of Pasternak's book. So what has this incident to do with the influence of literature?

From literature and politics, let me turn to drama and politics. I have had the lucky opportunity to observe at close range the most political of all modern dramatists, Bertolt Brecht. According to him, the drama was to be nothing if not social, and in an era like our own it was to do nothing if not contribute to social and revolutionary change.

Brecht was a far more gifted writer than Mrs. Stowe, yet can his contribution to history be considered any larger than hers? And, as with Pasternak, we must distinguish between the writer as a name to conjure with and the writer as mere writer. The name of Brecht was more valuable to the Communists than were the works of Brecht. Society's interest in art may be slight, yet society may at the same time accord prestige to the artist—just as one may revere a scientist like Einstein without having the least idea what he has done that deserves revering. The sociology of art should, I think, deal with such factors as these.

The theme of drama and propaganda is full of paradox. Brecht's intention had been to take art down a peg, and to model his work on science. Ultimately, his error was the usual one made by artists and critics of art: the over-estimation of art. For he attributed great political importance to the theatre, an institution that has very little effect on politics. Just as one can justifiably ask of someone who prefers Russia, why doesn't he go to Russia? so one can ask of someone who prefers science or politics, why doesn't he go into science or politics? A playwright with a few notions about Galileo is never going to match the scientists on their own ground.

The sobering, and perhaps shocking, fact is that

the artist has been and today remains a slave—or, if you prefer, a lackey. Communist critics have never tired of illustrating this fact with data from ancient, feudal and capitalist society. There was always the patron, and there is still the patron today, even though his name be hidden behind that of a newspaper or a magazine or a publishing house. What we have become acutely aware of since 1930 is that Communist countries—except in the performing arts—have made matters worse rather than better. In Western society one can at least become the lackey of some rebel prince—let's say of a millionaire who supports a Communist magazine. The fates of Meyerhold and Eisenstein tell us what happens to rebels in Russia.

We should not lose sight of the fact that the rebel artist plays just as subservient a role in rebellion as his brother plays in conservation. God help any regime—and God help any rebellion—that depends heavily on its artists! They are on the whole, not a dangerous lot, as Plato thought, but a useless lot. A brutal government might logically ship them off to forced labor—as one hears that the present Chinese government is doing.

I think, in short, that our exploration of drama and society should begin with the realization that there has been prevalent a gigantic illusion on this subject: the illusion that the artist is characteristically the master rather than the slave. Perhaps, of course, this is the characteristic illusion of the artist—whom sheer powerlessness drives to dreams of power. The image many people have of the artist as sublime and Promethean only holds for very great artists. The average artist is not a Prometheus but a Walter Mitty.

In approaching the subject of drama and society, I address myself first to propaganda, because it is through propaganda that drama most simply can cope with society. Yet even this relatively crude subject has its ambiguities as we have already been finding. The phrase "propagandist drama" suggests different things to different people. To most, perhaps, it suggests a drama that furthers social change and particularly total change or revolution. But, after all, the "other side" has its propaganda too, and plays can be written in the interests of the status quo: Shakespeare's histories are a case in point.

I am speaking of works which directly champion the preservation of the status quo, and implicitly recognize some threat to it. Works in which the status quo is merely accepted, and no alternative imagined, would not be propaganda unless we considerably extend the word's normal scope. Precisely this has been proposed by many people in the past fifty years—chiefly people influenced by

Marxism. There is the slogan: Art is a weapon. And one used to hear people say—perhaps one still would everywhere except in this country—All Art is Propaganda. Such a phrase has its utility in reminding us that even classic writers of wide academic acceptance had some axe to grind. It is still a little puerile to lump together in this way Clifford Odets' *Waiting for Lefty* and Dante's *Divine Comedy*. So I will hold to the older understanding of the word as implying a direct effort at changing history, if, in some cases, only a little bit of history. For example, a work which seeks to convert you to a religion is propaganda. A work which merely presents that religion, or embodies its author's belief in it, is not. Admittedly, a person might be converted by the second type of work, and it has often been urged with some justice that propaganda is bad propaganda: the proselytizer makes fewest proselytes. But this is to comment on the limitations of propaganda, not to change the definition of it.

It is commonly assumed, I think, that propaganda is fundamentally offensive rather than defensive. That is because only its offensives are visible. If one can generalize at all in this matter, I would say that the stance of the propagandist is a defensive one, and that, if he hits, it is only when he believes he is hitting back. The starting point is

E ciò sa il tuo Dottore.

a threat, real or imagined. Hitler's plot to take over the world is the dream of a man who felt persecuted. His persecutions are at once a revenge for and a forestalling of persecutions to himself, more imagined, of course, than real.

It is common, in this connection, to give the origin of the word: *congregatio de propaganda fide,* a committee of Cardinals who were given charge of propagating the faith. If we stop here, we might make shift with the positive conception of the process and the impulse that leads to it. The date when the congregation was set up tells us otherwise. It is 1622—at the height of the counter-Reformation. What brought this, the original, propaganda into being was the threat of Protestantism. From the counter-Reformation on, the word propaganda has kept the connotation of fanaticism, or at least zeal. It is the work of men in a tremendous hurry, which they believe is imposed on them by events. Propaganda is a weapon, and it is an emergency weapon, one to use when police methods have failed. When literature won't work, so to say, you may be forced to try propaganda. One sees writers reaching this conclusion whenever there's a war on. And always with us are people who say there's already a war on, and so the time for the use of this heavy artillery is now. "It's later than you think!" Act before it is too late!

This assertion, which prompts propaganda in the first place, is nowadays its content, too. And again one would have to point to the illusion of believing that the propaganda makes very much difference. Brecht said, in effect, that you don't paint a still-life when the ship is going down. He seems not to have realized that you don't paint at all when the ship is going down. A few artists *have* voluntarily given up their art in view of the urgency of a social situation, but if all artists were so consistent, propagandist art would be self-liquidating. At this point one sees that emergency art is based not only on an illusion but also on a bit of trickery. The ship is going down, and though one hasn't time to paint a still-life, one has time to paint a picture of ships that are going down because the ship owners want to collect the insurance. This picture is justified by its future utility, but actually took as long to paint as a still-life. If that utility is imaginary, the whole operation stands revealed as a double cheat. Meanwhile, the artist has brought painters of still-lifes into disrepute, while securing automatic praise for his picture of a shipwreck on the grounds of its urgency, utility, rightmindedness and so forth.

I am giving in a parable the story of social art in our time. And don't let anyone say that it all passed away in the Thirties. More to the point is that what we call here the spirit of the Thirties is now strong in Western Europe, while something not unlike it is sweeping Asia and Africa. So much for what is wrong with the whole notion of propaganda in art.

I have been talking as if a work were either pure propaganda or not propaganda at all. Yet the propaganda in Shakespeare's histories has lost all its urgency and some of its plausibility, while the plays remain alive because they have the virtues of good plays of the non-propagandist sort. An author may intend a piece of propaganda, and inadvertently produce a work of art. Or he may have two separate intentions, in conflict or in harmony. It is a complex and mixed phenomenon.

One should distinguish, too, between preaching to the converted and preaching to the heathen. The original Congregation of Propaganda was dedicated to the conversion of the heathen. And a pattern of social drama that existed in the Nineteen Thirties showed an irresolute person, characteristically a liberal, being forced into choosing between Communism and Fascism and choosing or failing to choose the former. Here the old reversal at the center of a plot is combined with a quasi-religious conversion. The real question—whether a person *is* forced into that particular dilemma—is begged. Propaganda was never strong on philosophy—the point is "not to understand the world but to change it." Dramaturgically, one might say that the skill in manipulating situations which is usually applied frivolously is in propaganda plays applied unscrupulously, as by a Machiavellian or Jesuitical extremist. Certainly the type of drama that is addressed to the task of converting people seldom tries to do it by reason. If you proceeded by pure reason, you wouldn't invoke the aid of theatre in the first place: another point overlooked by Bertolt Brecht, who often thought of theatre as being as rational as a laboratory. But Brecht was consistent at least to the extent of writing only one straight conversion play, *Señora Carrar's Rifles.* Since his own more characteristic type of drama was devised to deal with our modern emergency, it is curious that he gives this emergency as his pretext for reverting to conventional drama in the play I am speaking of.

I suppose Bernard Shaw has come closer than anyone else to writing plays calculated to persuade. At least we think of him as such a playwright. Coming down to cases, we perhaps have only one play to come down to, and it is only part of a play at that: the Don Juan scene from *Man and Superman.* That is a piece of persuasion if there is a piece of persuasion in all of world drama. But is it actually persuasive? By this, I don't mean: was Shaw right? I mean: even assuming he was right, are the tactics of this masterpiece calculated to win over someone who disagrees? One assumes that Shaw agrees with Don Juan. Yet he also gives the Devil his due. Don Gonzalo and Ana do not argue, but they embody parts of human life not embraced by the Don. A favorable response to the play is not likely to take the form of feeling won over. Rather, we feel we have shared a noble vision of life. And that is another way of saying we have taken the scene to be, not propaganda, but drama.

There exists a series of works which are persuasive but are not quite dramas: Plato's dialogues. I go by fairly orthodox definitions. Shift the normal definitions, as Georg Kaiser did, and Plato's dialogues can be the quintessence of drama. They certainly have many of the obvious characteristics of the dramatic form, and the death of Socrates can be presented on stage as a tragedy with very little changing of the text. Are Plato's dialogues propaganda? Again, it is, in the first instance, purely a semantic question. I have suggested that urgency—a plan for immediate, overt change—belongs to the definition. That is why I couldn't include Plato among the propagandists. That is also why practical persons call him a Utopian.

Not very much writing actually tries to persuade, though quite a lot pretends it does. We are familiar with this kind of pretense from conversation and oratory. The motions of persuasion are gone through, but the audience actually envisaged is already persuaded. Before an audience of fellow Republicans, a Republican gives his answer to the Democrats—a different thing indeed from a Republican's persuading a Democrat to be a Republican. Much drama that makes controversial points relies, without ever admitting it, on the audience's prior agreement. No Broadway play about Negroes tries to persuade a conservative Southerner he is wrong. Every such play seeks to confirm the anti-Southern Northerner in what he already feels. Hence, what is called the "boldness" in the presentation calls for no boldness in the author. On the contrary it tempts him toward demagogic self-congratulation.

Is there a propagandist drama which is deliberately addressed to those who are already convinced? Certainly. Under this head comes religious drama addressed to a particular denomination, or political drama addressed to a particular party. Here the issue is not the truth or untruth of the cause but only its celebration and its defense. Shakespeare put no case for nationalism in *Henry V*. He addressed his fellow nationals and fellow nationalists and called them to a feeling of solidarity—called them also to hatred of the French. The religious drama of the Middle Ages is not propagandist at all under the definition I am following, because it is not defensive. The religious drama of the Spaniards in the seventeenth century is often another matter: it is the literature of the counter-Reformation.

In most of the liberal and leftwing drama of our days there are ambiguities. Some of it might be read as an attempt by Communists to make converts of liberals. But something like a trick, and a double trick at that, was often played. The author didn't admit to his Communism. At the same time he strongly implied that the progressive view, as currently accepted by the Party, is already acknowledged as truth by any rightminded person—so no good man really needs any converting in the first place.

The equivocation invades even the writing of professed Marxists and fellow travelers like Brecht. A certain amount of deliberate falsification was involved. For example, Brecht once wrote a scene to show that the Communists and Social Democrats continued to fight even when they were fellow prisoners in Nazi camps. On the advice of a better Communist than himself, he changed the scene to say just the opposite. The facts of the camps had not changed, but it was wartime, and the policy was a united front against Hitler. A useful lie was told; but what, actually, was its usefulness? Not, obviously, that very many people took Brecht's word for it and said: we can all sink our differences and fight Hitler. That is a supposed reason which few will accept as the real one. The actual effect was to give an impression that Marxist theory was softening in view of the fact that Bertolt Brecht no longer saw Social Democrats as the enemy.

If Brecht's plays are taken as argument they must often be taken as arguing in a circle. What is proved at the end of *The Good Woman of Setzuan* is assumed at the beginning, and no fact is presented along the way except as exemplifying the initial assumptions.* Brecht says: "These are the facts—and look what follows from them." Anyone is free to reply: "If those were the facts, those would be the consequences. But those are not the facts." In short, Brecht really had in mind an audience of people who wouldn't question his version of the facts. There is no exploration in any of his plays of what the facts are. The truth is something established before the first line is written. The questions that arise are questions like: Will a person (his St. Joan) come to see this truth? Is a person (Galileo) strong enough to stand by this truth?

* But see page 221 below.

Brecht is said to have declared himself the last Catholic playwright, and certainly one remarks his tendency to write about martyrs of his faith. Doubts about the faith are seen, not as possibly reasonable differences in opinion, but as signs of personal inadequacy or outright cowardice. To make this point, Brecht attributes to Galileo views he could never possibly have held. The thesis is: Galileo held a modern progressive's view of history and even doubted the existence of God: if he didn't say so, it is because he was afraid of instruments of torture.

We have also seen in our time a revival of drama in the churches. Not much of it is propaganda in my definition, but I was surprised to hear T. S. Eliot say not long ago that *Murder in the Cathedral* was intended to be propaganda against the Nazis. His Becket was meant, apparently, as a sort of Pastor Niemöller in conflict with the state. Curious that such an intention should be revealed only years later, as in a note explaining an obscure line of *The Waste Land*. Anti-Nazi propaganda could scarcely be effective if kept such a closely guarded secret.

How effective is *any* propaganda in the theatre? I have already expressed my skepticism about propaganda generally. I can hardly waive it in this instance. What *Murder in the Cathedral* could have done against the Wehrmacht and the SS would in any event have been negligible. Persuasion, we have seen, is seldom attempted and, when attempted, seldom succeeds. With pretended persuasion, we come to propaganda drama that is really addressed to those already convinced. What can religion do for the converted—by theatrical means? and in the way of propaganda? The aim would be to fill with emotional content what may otherwise be a feebly "intellectual" tenet. You are made to feel strongly about a certain thing, and if the dose is repeated often enough, your feeling will perhaps harden into a habit. One believes this; yet one cannot measure any of the factors involved. For example, the theatre might help to inculcate patriotism, but if a theatre-goer is a patriot, how can you tell how much of his patriotism actually comes from the theatre? I cannot imagine any attitude becoming socially important unless many more people than the dramatists are fostering it.

I speak, of course, from a twentieth-century background. The drama is now surrounded by radio, movies and TV. Things were different in the days when the theatre was the principal source of entertainment. Yet even then the home, the church and the school were more important training grounds. Our Puritan forebears thought the theatre more likely to be a place where wisdom is unlearned. They had a good deal of evidence to go on.

We cast about for big claims to make. The arts seem to prompt people to grandiose pronouncements. Threatened, we make propaganda for theatre—as well as demand a theatre of propaganda. We even read in the papers that in asking some millionaire for money to build a theatre, a high-minded managing director has offered him in return all manner of high ideals. If a New York impresario wants to show us the Comédie Française, he starts to burble about international peace, and we have visions of general disarmament resulting from transatlantic crossings.

The theme of drama and society suggests to me, in the first place, some of these big claims and, in the second place, their falsity. They can, of course, be understood. I think they belong to a phase of American evolution, and maybe of world evolution, in which masses of people are having their first inkling that the arts might be a good thing and might even enter their lives. I myself come of unlettered parents who, when they gave me an education, had to envisage the arts I studied on the analogy of religion. Their religion being evangelical, like most of the religion of England and America, they thought of the arts as being the way their son would do good to people, and perhaps abolish war, not to mention drunkenness. And I might confess also that, as I had been intended for a missionary of the church, I find it hard at times not to see myself as a missionary of culture.

Then there is the guilt we all feel, or have felt, at the fact that we are fiddling while Rome burns. The impulse to join Schweitzer in Africa, or Klaus Fuchs in East Germany, is felt by more people than actually do it. Many have tried to appease their guilt by saying: I will practice the kind of art that helps democracy, or that helps Stalin, or that helps God.

This making of excessive claims for art comes, oddly enough, from having too little faith in it. We search far afield for its purpose only because we cannot look it in the face. It is to gain the whole world for us, because it has lost its own soul. What worries us is the modesty, the intimacy of art as it really is: its real effects are small, internal, personal and hard to describe or even to observe. Hence, though the purpose of the Ninth Symphony may be to introduce universal brotherhood, the chilling fact is that it has failed to do so. Shall we join the Salvation Army which undoubtedly has more success in that direction? I would respect the man who drew such a conclusion more than the man who trumpets that our modern artists must strive to succeed where Beethoven failed.

There is a third possibility: to find what the Ninth Symphony can actually do for people—what it has done for some and will do for others. What actually happened to you when last you heard that work may seem rather a small incident compared with the invention of the atom bomb, but must you have an inferiority complex about this? The arts depend for their existence on our respect for such small incidents. I believe that the exploration of drama and society must properly start from respect, not for society, but for the individuals whom it comprises, and in the first instance, for their private experience. Secondly, artistic activity must be taken as a good in itself and therefore not needing justification on grounds of its utility in other fields, such as religion or politics. It satisfies a natural and not unhealthy craving. It is part of the good life. It is not suspect. It need not be on the defensive. If these two points—which are really one—are accepted, we must conclude that whatever, if anything, the arts may do for a society, they make a contribution to the life of individuals.

PRO

But aren't the arts social—and not just in the sense that society is made up of individuals? The

question is unmanageably large but it will be help-
ful, perhaps, to note that the various arts vary
greatly in the degree of their "sociability." While
lyric poetry is presumably the least social of the
arts, drama is very likely the most social of them
all. For a play in performance (how often we hear
it!) is the fruit of a collaboration among many,
and it is then presented to many more, who sit as a
crowd before it and lose, in some measure, their
individual identity. "Sociability" permeates theatrical life.

It is true that critics of theatre have grossly exaggerated its crowd psychology to the end of defend-
ing their anti-intellectual outlook, yet the theatre
is sociable—even in ways they seldom mention. For
example: when you wish to enjoy art alone, you
read a book. You go to the theatre when you wish
to enjoy it in company with someone else—not so
much all those strangers in the other rows as the
friends in your own party. Theatre is not necessarily a mass meeting: it *is* necessarily a gathering.
There is no maximum size for an audience, but I
would say the minimum is two. To relish theatre,
you have to relish enjoying an art together with at
least one other person. Even the critic who revels
in his detachment from the audience as a whole is
much influenced by his wife—not necessarily by
her opinions (for he is a subtle fellow and on

guard) , but certainly by her smiles, her scowls and her murmurs of: Really! Such influence is not any less when it works in reverse. The critic who hates his wife reverses the judgments that he judges her to have made.

If theatre, like other arts, feeds the inner life of individuals, more than other arts it depends for its existence on groupings, or societies, of individuals. The theatre is a society within society. And a theatre is created by persons who feel the need to create a society with society—a refuge, if you like, a haven, a little world. That is the smallest thing a theatre can be. At certain moments in history the theatre has been more. Though still physically small at these moments, it is a match for society as a whole. The people is its audience, and the life of the people is seen steadily and whole in its dramas. Such was the miracle of fifth-century Athens or seventeenth-century Spain.

You cannot create those moments by wanting to. They were created by a confluence of many circumstances, most of them outside the drama itself. Much has been written about the changes that have come about since the seventeenth century, but it is well to recall that even before that there were few ages of great drama. Nor must we assume that the drama necessarily has an endless future. Artistic forms come and go more quickly than biological species. With these cautions in mind, let us turn to our situation today.

The world is in a troubling but fascinating period of transition between aristocratic culture and a culture that will be in some sense of the term democratic. It is surely not surprising if many features of this transition are bizarre or just plain deplorable, yet people who cite the bizarre and deplorable things nearly always assume that aristocratic culture was characterized throughout by truly aristocratic qualities. What about the aristocrats of tsarist Russia? They are depicted by the aristocrat Leo Tolstoy in his novel *Resurrection*. The aristocrats of nineteenth-century England were characterized by Matthew Arnold as the Barbarians. Milton described those of the seventeenth century as drunk with insolence and wine. Mozart's life was one long indignity as a result of their callousness and stupidity.

True, those who hoped for a flowering of culture with the onset of democracy have been disappointed. They supposed that once the working man had leisure, he would take to arts and crafts; and actually he takes to automobiles and television. Some people will never recover from their surprise and disgust at this fact. That is why they either refuse to contemplate any more heartening phenomena, or hasten to "explain" them. The ex-

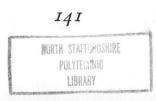

plaining is mere explaining away, as when one is invited to attribute the new mass interest in classical music to the personal glamor of Mr. Leonard Bernstein. And why must we cast a cold eye on personal glamor? Mr. Bernstein makes the wide public feel welcome in the halls of culture. Is that bad? On the contrary, it helps us to see that what stood between that public and the enjoyment of great music was partly a social apparatus that made them feel excluded. Opera and symphony were addressed to dowagers. The working man didn't have the right clothes for the occasion, or the right accent, or the right kind of chit-chat. Invited to a concert, he could hardly be expected to feel like anything but a pariah.

Much the same is true of theatre. In America that institution is still amazingly upper-class in its mores, and extraordinarily inconvenient in its prices and its schedule for anyone who earns a modest living. How true this is one only realizes fully when the prices and the schedule and the social atmosphere abruptly change, as they did on the creation of the Federal Theatre in the Thirties. Millions of Americans who "never go to the theatre" suddenly went to the theatre.

It is easy to be overcome with gloom as we contemplate the recent history of what has come to be called Mass Culture. Indeed, stronger than all the evidence provided by writers on the subject is the sadness in the writers themselves—covered though it conventionally is by a devastating smartness of tone. But the prospects for anything good are always black. The good things were often flatly impossible until they happened—it is only afterward that they were found to have been inevitable. If we bow to what is inevitable beforehand, what we are going to get is George Orwell's 1984. Still-lifes get painted by people who are determined to paint them even if they are on board ship and even if the ship is going down. Sometimes there are enough lifeboats. Sometimes land is in sight.

Alongside Broadway, alongside TV, there exists a certain hunger for high art. That does not mean that art is always liked, let alone understood. But one would have to be a fanatic pessimist to assert that it is uniformly disliked and misunderstood. Those of us who have a professional interest in culture are inclined to let our irritation at modern vulgarities blind us to any concomitant achievement. We are acutely aware, for example, that many of the classical phonograph records that are bought are not really listened to but are used as a background to work or conversation. We are less inclined to concede that some listening does occur. We note the incongruous context of classical paintings when they are reproduced in *Life* magazine.

We overlook the fact that a serious interest in painting might stem from a reading of *Life* magazine.

Or consider the notorious bad taste of the large public. One form it takes is that of a naïve earnestness which leads it to consider the latest domestic drama on Broadway as just as profound as Ibsen or even Shakespeare. Lionel Trilling recently made a cutting remark about the dramatists who write these plays of modern life. It was to the effect that he studiously refrains from seeing their work. The remark was, I think, a deserved rebuke to the pretentiousness of certain playwrights and to the ignorance of such devotees of theirs as do not know that the same sort of thing has been done much better by others. A play like *Death of a Salesman* gets to be taken more seriously than it deserves to be.

Mr. Trilling, I gather, sees the public's undiscriminating earnestness as a wholly negative factor and has proposed as a sort of alternative a light comedy called *Two for the Seesaw*. Here I believe his sophistication has betrayed him. The fact that he will see or read so few Broadway plays has permitted him to believe that *Two for the Seesaw* has considerable distinction. It really hasn't. Such items abound on the Broadway program, and when you've seen three, you've seen the lot. More important: the earnestness which Mr. Trilling rejects out of hand is not all bad. At bottom it is a demand for high seriousness and as such not only a good thing but a supremely encouraging thing to anyone with the interests of high theatre at heart. It is because this demand is imperious—because the public will not take No for an answer—that something has to present itself as Highly Serious several times every season. Much is passed off as sublime that is in fact only earnest—something that no one has failed to notice who has given Broadway more than a cursory look. The public, as is well known, is likely to find *Death of a Salesman* just as noble and profound as *King Lear*. The invalidity of this proposition has prevented critical people from seeing the corollary: *King Lear* is just as noble and profound as *Death of a Salesman*—in other words, the mass public has nothing, finally, against *King Lear,* but is willing to be as moved and impressed by it as by a much more easily accessible modern work.

In the cultural revolution that is under way all over the world, the theatre could play a leading part for the reason that high theatrical art is more accessible to the new untrained audiences than perhaps any other high art whatsoever. Most of music and painting is inaccessible except to people of a certain training. The same is true of poetry.

Fiction is a little more approachable. I know people who left school at thirteen whose reading for pleasure embraces most of Tolstoy. And the drama —not in its printed form, but on the stage—is the most accessible of all high arts. That fact seems to me to give it a certain responsibility. And here I do not have in mind a drama that is in any intentional or overt way didactic. I am thinking, rather, of plays that speak to the heart. But then all good plays speak to the heart, not least those of the supposedly cerebral playwrights, such as Shaw. The masterpieces of dramatic art may have subtleties in them that it takes generations of scholars to decipher. They certainly have a characteristic that is far more important socially: they are emotionally powerful, and their principal emotions are such as make an immediate impact on a crowd. I think one might even say that the subtleties are at the periphery and that the center of each great drama is a certain simplicity. I do not, of course, mean superficiality, but rather that inessentials are so fully eliminated that we face an elemental and universal subject in its nudity. In this sense, the story of the Crucifixion is simple as told in the Gospels, even though men still disagree as to what it means.

One of the most sophisticated of modern plays is Pirandello's *Henry IV* and much has been written of its philosophy. At the core of the play, however, is something that all men feel keenly about: growing old. This is a play about a man of forty who clings to the image of himself at twenty. That is to say: this is a play about Everyman. Writing for a literary magazine, you assume that this fact is clear to all and you proceed to argue about the philosophy; and many writers for literary magazines come to identify the non-obvious with the essential. A theatre audience does the opposite, and is, I think, less wrong. Certainly, it has a better starting point for judgment: with the primary emotional experience. *King Lear* may contain all manner of Elizabethan lore concerning kingship for scholars to talk about. But if they have not started from actually feeling what Shakespeare says here about fathers and children, they have not started from the center. A public that picked up the points about parents and children would have responded more properly to the play than one that picked up points about Elizabethan culture. And that is understating my thesis, for it is not really a matter of points to be picked up, but of spontaneity versus sophistication. You hear a Beethoven quartet by having a sensibility and listening, and not by knowing things about Beethoven and about quartets.

As for great drama, I am saying something even

simpler: that while there are barriers between it and the great public, these barriers can often be broken down by the fact of theatre, the act of performance. And that without any jazzing up or deliberate popularization. Literary people complain that in performance the subtle passages whizz past before one can take them in. For non-literary people that is an advantage. A play whose value lies in the subtlety of separate passages is not a popular play. Nor have any plays of that sort ever, I think, been considered great. When a subtle play is popular it is because behind the subtlety lies a human simplicity, a limited number of universal and powerful emotions. People will tolerate any amount of subtlety provided they can ignore it, and they can ignore it with pleasure if they are borne along by even one unsubtle, strong emotion. In the theatre, who ever notices that the first act of *Hamlet* contains much more information than we can retain? We are preoccupied by the one, simple, central situation: the death of the father, the re-marriage of the mother, the desolation of the son, the appearance of the father's ghost.

"Theatre," notoriously, is mostly mass entertainment of low artistic quality. Some mass entertainment is of high artistic quality—one thinks of some of the comedians who have been the darlings of the modern masses—but, by and large, the artistic theatre is a thing apart for people with not only an education but a special interest or hobby. This apartness implies a division in modern society as a whole and has been widely discussed in such terms as highbrow and lowbrow. The discussions are unpleasant. Both high and lowbrows have ferocious champions, and the middlebrows, as becomes them, have milder ones—or perhaps only snider ones. No real discussion is possible because the statements of the various teams imply accusations that are also insults. The champion of the highbrows implies that his opponents have no taste. The champion of the lowbrows implies that his opponents are undemocratic—the most violent epithet in the American vocabulary.

I have contributed on the highbrow side to this polemic. But the returns are not all in. Much has yet to be learned about the nature of popular taste, as also about the possibilities of so-called highbrow theatre among those presumed to be lowbrows. When this kind of theatre was suddenly made available in America at prices the mass audience could pay, and in places where the mass audience lives, the mass audience attended the theatre and paid. I refer again to the Federal Theatre. Jean Vilar has been having "highbrow" successes with huge popular audiences in France, and has also been making discoveries about popular predilections. His audiences like best the plays which are not of the type known as popular. They like the plays they are supposed to dislike. A prime instance is Kleist's *Prince of Homburg*. Frenchmen don't like Germans, especially not Prussians, and especially not Prussian Junkers; but Kleist was a German and a Prussian and a Junker and suddenly this play of his, considered in German to be esoteric, appeals to a mass audience in France. I should add that it was produced with the greatest possible austerity—that is, quite without all the devices of deliberate "popularization." Another case in point is that of Paul Claudel. To the Communist press, he is a Catholic apologist, and the working-class audience in France is powerfully influenced by the Communist press. Claudel's style, furthermore, is what an English critic has called Mandarin—it bears all the marks of the highbrow caste. Yet the plays of Claudel have been captivating mass audiences in France.

Various conclusions could be drawn. What occurs to me is that, though the motive of going to the theatre is "to be entertained," a great deal more than entertainment may be painlessly added. The common man's demand not to be bored is a reasonable one. But once you have succeeded in not boring him, you have indeed "captivated" him: you can do what you want with him and he may even approve. For it is possible that, once relieved of boredom, even the least artistic person wants to be treated as a work of art will treat him. After all, it is not necessarily the substance of a great work that the public fears. People who cannot read Racine may just be scared of verbiage— look at the endless lines, lines, lines! The passions which are the real substance of Racine are not rejected—they are unperceived.

Despite the movies, radio and TV, there is still a lot of interest in the theatre. Indeed, it has never conclusively been shown that this interest has declined. Losses in one respect seem to have been recouped in another.

I want to make a suggestion which is almost practical. Leaving alone the kind of theatres we already have, I think it is desirable to add to them certain theatres in which great drama is produced for popular audiences. This has already been attempted more than once, but in most cases there has been what I have just called deliberate popularization. That is, the producers did not trust to the primary emotions of the classics—or their great universal themes—to put the material across. They relied on external devices, and particularly on the red pencil. The text was cut to ribbons, and what was left was arbitrarily modernized. If, before bringing a classic before the public, you convert it into just another modern entertainment, what point are you making? That the public doesn't like the classics? Quite often, for that matter, the public hasn't taken to the modern improvements.

You can set a Shakespeare story in present-day Texas or Edwardian England, but you cannot thereby hide the tameness of tame acting. Conversely, if the acting is not tame, it does not need such external aids to success.

Yet how often our failures are misinterpreted! "Shakespeare won't 'go' even when you give 'em Texas costumes"—etcetera. It has not occurred to people who say such things that the Texas costumes might be worse than a waste of money—that they might positively hamper the show. But I don't wish to make much of even that possibility. Even with Texas costumes Shakespeare could be well acted and so win its audience. I am saying we should place our faith in the power of the writing and the power of the acting. My almost practical proposal, then, is for the creation of troupes which will perform the classics for popular audiences but will address themselves wholly to the best possible performance, ignoring entirely what is called popularization. I think my point has already been granted in the realm of music. Any good conductor would give the same performance of the Ninth

Symphony before a mass audience that he would give before fellow musicians. He would see no alternative to just doing his best.

What of dramatic literature? That propaganda falls far short of its objectives—we are speaking of the propaganda of artists, not of politicians and advertising men—is no reason why an artist should not be moral, or even didactic. It is not even a reason why he shouldn't write propaganda if that's what he wants to do—a comment I make uncynically, meaning thereby that, ultimately, artists do what they can't help doing, whether it works or not. In any event, an artist cannot give up regarding himself as the conscience of mankind, even if mankind pays no attention.

Will what we have all called the Social Drama have a future? First, perhaps, it should be established what we have—or should have—meant by the term. If, as is sometimes said, all drama is social, then the expression has indeed no value. Nor is there much more point in using the word "social" as an accolade and awarding it, as Arthur Miller does, to all the plays one approves of. It makes more sense to reserve it for its usual application—that is, to plays which are, in their main emphasis, political, sociological. The Germans have a term, *Zeitstück,* for a play that tries to cope with a problem of the day. A leading playwright, I believe, might be expected to cope with *the* leading problem of the day. It will, of course, be of the highest interest *what* he considers that problem to be.

There exists the possibility that the leading problem of the day cannot be coped with at all—at any rate by playwrights. One of our playwrights has, in fact, taken the position that it cannot. "The world of today," writes Friedrich Dürrenmatt, "cannot be envisioned because it is anonymous and bureaucratic. . . . Creon's secretaries close Antigone's case." And yet Dürrenmatt writes plays, and these plays do present what the author quite evidently intends as an image of the characteristic reality of our time. The essay I have just quoted from also contains this avowal: "Any small-time crook, petty government official or cop better represents our world than a senator or president. Today art can only embrace the victims, if it can reach men at all."

A rejoinder to Dürrenmatt's essay was written by Brecht himself. Brecht said the world of today could be mirrored on stage if it was presented as alterable. Such was the softened version he gave in 1955 of the belief he had held since 1928 that a playwright could present life in our time only with the help of Marxism.

Both playwrights need the formula: Today art

can only. . . . Both make, in effect, the statement: "On the face of it, the world of today simply cannot be got on to a stage. And yet it can: with the help of *my* philosophy." Since both of these dramatists have written social drama of some distinction, one could argue that both are right—and that perhaps a third playwright could turn the trick with a third philosophy. Which amounts to saying that both are wrong, and that it was not the rightness of the philosophy in question that wrought the miracle. *Mother Courage,* to take an example, is one of the best social dramas of the century. Marxism enabled Brecht to state in this play that war is the continuation of capitalism by other means. But is it this statement that interests any admirer of the play? Is it this statement, even, that makes us feel the play is burningly relevant? On the contrary, it is the fact, admitted by all philosophers and non-philosophers, that war has become the supreme problem of our society. When the play urges that simple fact, it speaks to the whole audience. When it links that fact to a particular sociological theory, it speaks to theorists—in the gray language of theory. Both Brecht and Dürrenmatt seem to tell us that it is as doctrinaires that they will survive. Their plays tell us another story.

The problem of poverty is now eclipsed by the

problem of atomic war; nor can most of us agree that the two problems are one. A new orientation is called for; one can even see it coming. In its 1959 Christmas issue, the socialist *New Statesman* featured a cartoon in which the stable of Bethlehem cowered beneath a super-store selling TV sets and streamlined cars with fins. A board read: We Never Had It So Good. Now when a radical cartoonist protests, not against poverty, but against prosperity, a landmark has been reached in the history of radicalism. At this point much of the old social drama becomes obsolete.

Not just the drama of the virtuous poor versus the wicked rich. Although war remains an issue, has in fact become *the* issue, many of the old war plays are obsolete. There is a theme in Brecht's war plays, including *Mother Courage,* that is as dead as a doornail: the theme of jingoism, the idea that what endangers the peace is the gleam of swords and the glamor of uniforms. The illusion that war is fun has gone. The only sword that now has symbolic value is the sword of Damocles.

And yet *Mother Courage* has a validity, which stems, not from "Das Lied vom Weib und dem Soldaten," but from the direct portrayal of a devastation distinctly similar to that of Hiroshima. Which is to say that the valid part of this "social drama" is not optimistic; but there is no need to describe it as pessimistic either. We have to do here with a vision of horror which is a vision of truth and therefore necessary to any sane outlook, stormy or serene.

Atomic explosion: there will be plays about what it means to live under this particular mushroom. We must expect a literature of terror and defeat, which is to say, of nihilism. Insofar as the artist in our time simply sits and broods, he will write *Waiting for Godot* and *The Chairs*. Is sitting and brooding satisfactory? Is it even preferable to Stalinism? (The question, for Brecht, for instance, was not a rhetorical one.) And yet: what else is possible? A few years ago men hoped to remake the world. Nothing short of that seemed worth exerting oneself for. Now we would be happy to stop the world from destroying itself. Do we think we can? And do we really want to?

To ask such questions is to realize that while war is the immediate problem, the ultimate problem is: what would we do with peace? A generation ago the liberal movement answered: "Feed the poor. Whatever is done about freedom, let the poor be fed." Sometimes the poor were fed; and always freedom was sacrificed. The reorientation that is at hand today will entail placing the question of slavery and freedom again at the center of liberal (radical, revolutionary) activity, especially intellectual activity. For, as Camus said in Stockholm, "the nobility of our calling will always be rooted in two commitments . . . the service of truth and the service of freedom."

The literature of freedom—our generation's literature of freedom, I mean—began as a response to a situation not unlike that of today. As the whole world now lives trembling beneath the shadow of a bomb, so Frenchmen of the Resistance lived from 1941 to 1943 under what seemed the shadow of final Nazi victory. The literature of what may then have seemed a special situation has now become the literature of the universal situation. As certain Frenchmen in 1942 had to regard the future as black, yet fought, regardless, against enslavement, so the writer today, unable to see through that mushroom cloud to the light of the sun, can proclaim his faith in that light, can struggle toward that light.

(1960)

AFTERTHOUGHT, 1967

When the avowals of the first part of this essay gave offense—as they did both to pro- and anti-Communist readers—I realized that this was because the second part does not meet the arguments of the first point for point, does not, perhaps, even balance the first in weight of logic and evidence. I knew I would have to give the whole subject further thought and proceed to conclusions which, in 1960, I had not reached. Such conclusions are to be found below in the title essay of the book.

Oddly enough—if it really is odd—in that title essay I take a position that is haughtily dismissed in the first part of the present essay without being vindicated in the second: namely, that "propagandist" literature can be not only healthy and inevitable (as is conceded), but also useful and even politically necessary. It is not that one's philosophy of literature changes of itself: my respect for the great body of art which is not propagandist is undimished. It is a matter of events outside literature. "Urgency" is not to be swept aside as the Con part of me swept it aside in this essay. Also, I think even the unpolitical poetry of, say, Robert Lowell will be the more vital because of the commitment he made to the Vietnamese people in 1966.

"The illusion of believing that the propaganda makes very much difference": if my Con spokesman was to bandy phrases like this, my Pro spokesman should have reminded him that even to make a very little difference can be a very big achievement, necessary to a social cause as well as to one's personal honor.

LETTER TO A WOULD-BE PLAYWRIGHT

ONE DOES NOT write on theatre without receiving letters from playwrights. There is the playwright who tells me I have all the right ideas about drama and he has put all these ideas into a play—will I read it? There is the playwright who gets his attorney to write me demanding that every copy of my review of his play be removed forthwith from the market or he will sue me. Most ingratiating of all is the playwright who hasn't yet written a play and wants to know how to write one. I always feel that, if I really knew the answer, I would myself be the author of a list of plays at least as good as *Oedipus Rex, King Lear* and *Phèdre*. But one such "playwright" recently raised questions I can at least begin to answer—as follows.

Dear X:

So you have not yet written a play. One could wish some of our other dramatists had shown equal restraint. But then, you tell me, you have not yet reached twenty. The temptation to write a play may well be on the point of becoming irresistible. Once it does so, all anyone can do is try to keep you from writing a bad play. It will not be easy. Many bad plays find favor in the great heart of the public, and most of them find favor in the heart, great or small, of their authors.

If you insist on writing a play, nothing can stop you from writing a bad one except the act of writing a good one. Can you learn to do this? Or, to give the question its classic form: can playwriting be taught? You tell me a friend of yours says it can't. But you tell *me* this because you assume that I believe it can. But do I? Well, yes and no, and more particularly—while I am feeling needled by your reading of my mind—No! There is a lot to be said for the unteachability of *any* subject. As I calm down, though, I shall agree with you in seeing no reason why playwriting should be regarded as *less* teachable than other subjects. Oh yes, it is less teachable than reading, writing and 'rithmetic, but those are elementary subjects. Play-writing is an advanced subject, and at the advanced stage in any field a student has chiefly to work on his own. The point is that while the teacher, at this stage, may intervene less often, his intervention may still be valuable, even, in certain cases, essential. A coach of professional swimmers does not jump in the water and manipulate his men's limbs. A psychoanalyst does not interrupt his patient's every third word. . . . In short, I would not exclude the possibility that a teacher might be useful to a playwright.

You tell me that even your friend who believes that playwriting *can* be taught adds that in practice it never is. Here my quarrel would only be with the word "never." I will grant you that most teaching of playwriting is ineffectual—if you will grant me that most teaching of everything else is ineffectual. Nature is said to be wasteful, but, if the art of education is anything to go by, art is even more wasteful. All these man-hours in class-rooms—for nothing—possibly for that worse than nothing which is miseducation—the kind that has to be unlearned later, if indeed it still can be! And the pity of it, considering that the children being miseducated are not idiots! The energy of youth passes through our schools like so much unused water power. The years of opportunity between

nine and nineteen are thrown away on mere sociability, and, of late, sociability has led through
boredom to unsociability, otherwise known as
crime. How can anyone believe in Education when
the educators have provided nothing but awful
examples of How Not To Do It?

But I hardly need to tell you what a mess education is: you are, after all, educated. Or does your
being educated *prevent* you from seeing the facts
of education as of everything else? How *have* you
spent the last ten years? On higher things, I should
judge, for your letter bears witness to your neglect
of lower things, notably grammar, syntax, diction,
not to speak of style. You cannot write English.
You propose to write plays; but you cannot write
English; and presumably you see no great contradiction here. You will tell me that English could
always be learned if absolutely necessary but that,
firstly, plays aren't written in the language of
Shakespeare, they are written in that of the gutter
and, secondly, plays aren't properly said to be written at all, they are constructed, a Wright not being
a Writer but an artificer, artisan or fixer.

The *reason* you will tell me this is that you
know I don't agree. You want to hear what I will
say because you smell a rat: you yourself don't
believe the stuff you are parroting. After all, you
have not yet taken that course in playwriting, and

so you are as yet incompletely indoctrinated with the anti-literary philosophy of its teachers. I will let you into the secret that underlies this philosophy—a secret deduction which perhaps those initiates don't even confess to themselves. It is this: because what is good as literature may be bad as theatre, it follows that bad writing is the first step to what is good in theatre. That is not undemocratic, you will admit: for such a first step can be taken by any citizen of whatever color, creed or race. Some citizens are even willing to pay tuition for the privilege.

Why not learn the tricks of a trade that is nothing but tricks? Well, there *is* a reason why not, and it is that the path of foolishness isn't always simple. Bad taste has its pitfalls, just like good. For that matter, who has the courage of his puerility? The fool must perforce deny being a fool. It is even true, despite Machiavelli, that the knave must deny—even to himself—being a knave. Conscious knavery such as Machiavelli recommended is as much of a strain as virtue. For the price, one might just as well be good. . . .

The teacher of play*wrighting* (despite Webster, it should be spelled that way) can start out cheerily enough with the declaration that the box office never lies, etcetera. The purpose of art is to please, etcetera. We aren't a lot of snobs, are we, etcetera.

Just look what awful plays those highbrows write, etcetera. Shakespeare, on the other hand, is one of us, he took a course in playwriting from the horses outside the Globe Theatre, etcetera. Oh, those awful literati, those coteries, those cliques, I wrote a play myself once, and you know what was done to me by those awful literati, those coteries, those cliques, etcetera? In short, what we believe in is Democracy, and the people's choice is made known to Brooks Atkinson at 11:30 every evening by a process which may be mystic but which is no less Real. Etcetera.

When the tumult and shouting die, you realize, I hope, that, of all the gods, the public is only a goddess and a bitch at that. La donna è mobile. If the public really ever had an opinion and stuck to it, one might at least be able to pay attention. But what is the public's verdict on *Abie's Irish Rose?* As of now, total indifference. As of thirty-five years ago, ecstatic approval. Now tell me—and don't use your head, use your public—is that a good play or isn't it? Don't bother to answer, just draw this moral: teachers who wish to teach the successful formulas are faced with the disturbing fact that the successful formulas change. It would even seem that a pattern sometimes fails precisely by becoming a formula, and has at that point to be replaced by another pattern, which in turn fails when it becomes a formula, and so on.

There is a bag of tricks in any profession, and young people will always learn the tricks, may often be the better for learning them and may never be the worse for learning them—provided they accept them at no more than their actual value. I am attacking—yes, now you have brought out the aggressor in me—the notion that a play differs from a poem or a picture precisely in being all tricks. No one ever put that notion forward, you say. Perhaps not, I reply, but the teachers imply its truth and not once or twice, but all the time. Upon that sand they have built their theatres. Upon pure philistinism. Upon hostility to sensibility and imagination, not to mention thought.

This is the real reason why the books on How To Write A Play are so depressing. In many of them there's a lot of shrewd observation. What worked last time is offered to the student as what is likely to work next time and a thousand times thereafter. A list of the things that worked last time—this kind of exposition, this kind of curtain line, this kind of leading character, this kind of ending—is known as Dramatic Technique, is known as How To Write a Play.

In time the books on How To Write a Play became a joke. It was then that the total unteachability of playwriting began to be talked about. No one can help you, because playwriting proceeds upon no principles! With the silly simple rules of the how-to books, these counter-revolutionaries throw out critical understanding altogether, falling back upon an extreme relativism—so many plays, so many rules—and an extreme subjectivism—each playwright a law unto himself. This philosophy, whatever its truth, is likely to be just as cramping as the how-to books themselves, for it gives the playwright nothing to lean on but Inspiration, a creature far too whimsical and elusive to keep him from the bottle.

Those who hold this view make the same mistake as those who hold the opposite: they conceive of playwriting as a thing apart, an art somehow exempt from the normal obligations of art. I want to start at the other end. The playwright is, first, an artist and, secondly, he is a particular kind of artist—a writer. This would be an utterly uncalled-for formulation were it not more and more assumed that the playwright is neither a writer nor an artist but only a manipulator.

Not long ago a playwright was summoned to the hotel room of a producer. The producer had read the script, and was proceeding not only to talk about it but to re-write it as he paced the carpet. He re-did the first scene on his feet, reciting all the roles. "You aren't taking it down," he then said to the playwright. "No," said the playwright. "I'm taking it in. I go home. I let all this rest in my mind. What I can't absorb evaporates. What remains gets into the play later—if I like it and know how to work it in. The play needs time for the absorption of the new ideas, the new material. These things must happen organically, sir." That playwright spoke as an artist and a writer. That producer spoke as a charlatan, not to say an egomaniac. The producer dropped the play on the grounds that the playwright didn't know his business. He meant, of course, that he didn't know his place. That place was the place of a stenographer—or shall we say an echo chamber for His Master's Voice? It isn't egomania I want to call your attention to, but the failure to cope with the psychology of the artist.

The artist has learned his craft but is never content to be a craftsman. The craft serves the art or, as Goethe put it, one only writes out of personal necessity. The endings of plays, for example, are not a gamble on the audience's response. They are a matter of what the playwright feels to be necessary. They cannot be open to discussion. Discussion with whom anyway? A work of art springs from its author's nature. No one can tell him what that is. Nor can he guarantee that any play he is working on will turn out well. That is where he differs from the craftsman. Craftsmanship can be perfected.

Consider what is happening when we take a work of art with a bad ending and stick on a good ending supplied to us by a craftsman or play-doctor. It can be true that we are perfecting the imperfect. I imagine a good craftsman could improve on the ending of Chekhov's *Ivanov*. However, from an artistic point of view, Chekhov's bad ending is necessary. The play could be fixed up externally with an ending that is neater and more logical, yet I don't think anyone could find an ending that would grow organically from the three preceding acts. If anyone could, he would be Chekhov's true collaborator—Beaumont to his Fletcher —and not a mere mechanic. It seems more likely that *Ivanov* is an impasse that can never become a thoroughfare. In *Ivanov* we have three superb acts from which there is no way out. When this sort of thing happens, an author writes another play. As for the public, it must settle for three great acts and accept one that is less than great.

If you have ever wondered why the newspaper critics often have more to say against the great writers than against the currently fashionable craftsmen, the example of *Ivanov* may make the reason clear. A craftsman can achieve a dead perfection. His work is the re-arrangement of known

elements—the solution of jigsaw puzzles. The artist's material is that greatest of mysteries, human
nature. He feels his way in the dark. In philistines
such things create anxiety and defensive resent-
ment, but for anyone in the audience who has an
inkling of what art is about, and an ounce of
sympathy for it, there is more enjoyment in the
imperfection of an *Ivanov* than in the bright, shal-
low perfections of the craftsmen.

Yet mustn't I get to know the theatre, you ask,
grease paint and gelatines, spots and teasers, flats
and wings—that celebrated other world behind
the footlights which is so notoriously "not literature"? I think you must. Or I *would* think you
must if your own letter did not suggest that you
already know that other world better than this
one. You certainly know more of theatre practice
than of literary practice. I think you should be
urged to restore the balance.

"Shakespeare and Molière . . ." you begin to
retort. I know. I have reason to know because I've
been told so often: Shakespeare and Molière were
actors. Molière was even a good actor. May *I* tell
you something about them which I can guarantee
you have not heard a thousand times before? They
both managed somehow to see a lot of the world
outside the theatre—of the two worlds outside the
theatre, in fact, the direct experience they had of
human living and the indirect experience of it that

is acquired through reading. Molière learned a lot
not only from clowns, but from Jesuits.

We have no certain knowledge of what Shakespeare was doing in the crucial decade of young
manhood, his twenties. There is an old tradition to
the effect that he was a teacher, though not of
playwriting. This tradition has been discounted
only because people haven't wished to believe in a
possibly erudite Shakespeare. Yet the plays themselves prove that he had studied and absorbed the
whole culture of his day. He was steeped in the
thought of his time as Thomas Mann, say, was
steeped in Freud. Freud, you tell me, is known on
Broadway too; he's even the only thinker who is.
Ah yes, but to be steeped in Freud, as Mann was,
is one thing, and to have dabbled a little in Freud-
ianism is to have acquired the little knowledge
that is worse than none.

Is there time, you ask, is there time to read more
than a little? Life is real, life is earnest, and one
ought to be seen a good deal at the Algonquin and
the Plaza. The smoke-filled room cannot also be
thought-filled,

> For at my back I always hear
> Time's wingèd chariot hurrying near . . .

And *Time* is as nothing compared to *The New
York Times*. The young playwright will be glad of
the help of more practical heads (arms, legs?)

from the Theatre. They can re-write him, right there in the hotel. In various hotels, changing with the stage scenery, New Haven, Boston, Philadelphia. . . .

To this, the answer is that more time would be left if less time were wasted. Every time-saving device from the telephone to the airplane ends up as a time-wasting device. The speeding-up of playwriting that takes place in hotels is a slowing-down of playwriting—in fact, a complete stoppage. Of course, it is true that playwrights must learn the art of the theatre, and above all its central art: that of acting. I would complain that most of them don't learn *enough* of it, partly because acting is a hard thing to learn about and very few people are especially sensitive to it, partly because the theatrical life generally consists in anything but the pursuit of essential theatre. It will be time to tell you to spend your days and nights with theatre people when theatre people spend their days or nights with the theatre art. At present, the injunction to be practical and get to know the working theatre is an injunction to squander the best years of your life in agents' offices, producers' offices, hotels, the right restaurants—or anywhere else in telephonic communication with these places.

We hear of the playwright's need of the theatre, but what of his need, equally real, to keep his distance? Henrik Ibsen "got to know the working theatre" as a young man, and that sufficed. To write plays, he went away from the theatre, nor did he return to see them through rehearsal. The most eminent of American playwrights, Eugene O'Neill, got his bellyful of theatre in childhood (maybe that's the best time), and considerably before middle-age he felt the need to put a healthy distance between himself and the gentlemen who know all about it. Even Bernard Shaw, who was sociable, and who liked to direct his own plays, took up residence, as soon as he could, out of reach of bus and train. Every morning, as long as he could walk, he went down to his garden hut. To write. In solitude.

Does that sound rather grim? If you think it does, then we are making an interesting discovery: that you are not a writer. You may want "the theatre," but what you do not want is to write. Either it must be some other theatrical job you are cut out for, or it is not even theatre you want: it is prominence or parties or la vie de bohème.

A writer, *qua* writer, does not "need the theatre." He only needs a typewriter, a table, a chair and, surrounding these objects, four walls and a door that locks. Even a hotel room will do, if the lock is a strong one and the phone is out of order.

Lonely? But isn't loneliness the modern writer's favorite subject? Should he belie its importance? Then again, what about "the lonely crowd"? It is visible enough on Times Square, and in all public buildings adjacent thereto. Solitude, in fact, can be borne only by those who suffer least from loneliness—by those, that is, who feel that their solitude is amply peopled. Writers are such persons. Their philosophy is that of Pirandello: people exist for you insofar as they have been taken into your thoughts and feelings. These thoughts and feelings stay on after the "people" leave the room. Amazing to think how crowded was the solitude of a Tolstoy or a Dickens! At the opposite pole, we have people whose solitude is a terrifying emptiness; it even hurts them that Sardi's is closed on Sunday.

Think about this when next you hear that some so-called writer is a "real man of the theatre." He may just be gregarious. Solitary work makes demands and he cannot meet them. Doubtless you remember Shaw's quip: those who can, do; those who cannot, teach. It requires but slight adjustment to our theme: those who can, write; those who cannot, write plays.

And those who cannot write plays, write television plays. The writer who cannot write is an institution nowadays, and makes more money than the writer who can write. Otherwise, why would he devote so much time to non-writing?

Do you want money? No, don't say anything. It really doesn't matter what a person *says* to that question. There are few persons who cannot be tempted by money. A poet is a person whose temptation to write poetry is so strong that it swamps the temptation to go after money. The poet has a simpler time of it than the dramatist: he makes a vow of poverty and leaves it at that. The dramatist never knows what will happen next. He may suddenly find himself as rich as the rich; but he cannot count on it. The situation is not easy on the nerves. Can *your* nerves stand it? And, if you did get rich, would you survive the experience as an artist? I am not assuming that you would wish to live like Aly Khan. I am thinking (among other things) of the following archetypal experience in twentieth-century America.

A man is born in the slums of Brooklyn or the Bronx. His writing is his response to that milieu. Broadway and Hollywood enable him to move to the East Sixties. It's only half an hour by cab from where the folks live, but, humanly speaking, it might as well be in outer space. Perhaps guilty conscience dictates a play saying how awful are the inhabitants of the East Sixties? But this play is not a good play. None of his plays are good plays any more. The theatre is now "hailing" a goodish play by a younger man—from Brooklyn or the Bronx—who is already in the taxi moving to the East Sixties.

I am (yes, you're right) only saying that, if you're going to be a writer, you will need a sense of identity. A firm one. Otherwise, "that undisturbed, innocent, somnambulatory process by which alone anything great can thrive is no longer possible." I am quoting a writer. He continues: "Our talents today lie exposed to public view. Daily criticisms, which appear in fifty different places, and the gossip that is provoked by them among the public, hamper the production of anything that is really sound. . . . He who does not keep aloof from all this and isolate himself by main force is lost." The author of *Egmont* and *Faust* is describing what would later be called the absorption of the intellectual by modern society. The creative process, he is saying, must not be disturbed, must not be deflowered. It must be a form of sleepwalking. Now Johann Wolfgang von Goethe was as worldly as any poet could afford to be. He spent much time on love affairs, and probably even more on affairs of state. But as for the world of the press agents and the press, he says: keep aloof or you will be lost.

Perhaps you are a stronger man than Goethe?

Let's assume you are strong enough to be a writer. That lonely room to which you are strong enough, and interested enough, to commit yourself must not be peopled exclusively with your personal memories. Nineteen years old as you are, you must not sit down and go to work without more ado on The Great American Play. Many have. And some of them have made a lot of money. What they have not made is The Great American Play.

In addition to memories, you need culture, all art being a crystallization of personal experience and second-hand experience. America is probably the only country in the world where a young person who wants to write a play (poem, novel) can imagine he is all set to go ahead on the basis of personal experience alone. (How many American short stories are but slightly more sophisticated renderings of the high-school theme, written in the autumn: Something That Happened To Me This Summer.) Everywhere else there is Culture. Which at its worst means: find out how it was done a hundred years ago and do it again, but at its best means: a sense of tradition.

A sense of tradition implies respect for the Masters. When the French actor Jean Vilar spoke in New York recently, many were surprised at his repeated allusions to "our fathers" and what they have left us. Where many Americans think they can "do it themselves" and deserve praise for trying to, your Frenchman unashamedly lives on inherited cultural wealth—without necessarily omitting to invest it properly and add the fruits of his own enterprise. Other Americans spend a good deal of emotional energy envying France. There is no need to; the Masters belong to all mankind. Among musicians, even in America, that fact is admitted. In the drama, as in all literature, there are language barriers. Yet have these stopped Balzac and Tolstoy from being an inspiration to novelists? *Per contra,* drama written in English—by Shakespeare—has inspired writers all over the world.

Why do the classics matter? They certainly do not perform all the functions that people have been pleased to assign to them. One could easily defend the thesis: The Classics Don't Work. They are nothing, or they are a fount of inspiration, especially to artists.

A few of the classics at a time, that is. For the artist is seldom a man of catholic tastes. Indeed it is doubtful if anyone really has the kind of taste which Higher Education supposes that he has: equally receptive to all kinds of greatness. If you are looking one way, you cannot be looking the other way; and a proper education would just help you to see, without claiming to give you eyes in the back of your head. To the artist, anyhow, the Masters are not a row of marble statues of equal size and indistinguishable features. Groupings and relationships change. Sometimes the artist must rebel against a particular Master, as the son against the father. There was Shaw's long campaign against Shakespeare. What one would deplore in a playwright would be indifference to Shakespeare, not hostility to him. In any case, Shaw was really attacking the public's attitude to Shakespeare rather than the man himself. Brecht later had to fight Goethe and Schiller. All that these things prove is that you can't have healthy religion without a certain amount of blasphemy.

The playwright's interest in the Masters is different from the scholar's interest. The scholar is concerned to place and appraise them. The artist is concerned only with what he can get out of them for his own practical purposes. His disrespect for information about them puts him at the opposite end of the scale from performers on a quiz program. But his need of the Masters is greater than anyone else's. They are his food. Goethe revealed to Eckermann that he could not let a year go by without reading some Molière.

It is hard, I think, for the aspiring American playwright to acquire such an attitude. I call your own letter to witness. "How," you rhetorically ask, "can one possibly imitate the classics today?" Who asked you to? Why so defensive? Stravinsky doesn't imitate earlier music. He makes legitimate use of it. And you might give a little thought to Bertolt Brecht's use of *The Beggar's Opera*—except that it is not so much the direct exploitation of classics that you need to know about at present as their subtle, indirect, pervasive, fructifying force.

It is not just a matter of the Masters. It is a matter of the relation between the playwright and the whole past of the art he serves. That relationship is always important and has in our time become even more so.

The last hundred years has seen the attempt to create a new kind of theatre that is the reverse of classic in any of the accepted senses of the term. The aim of the new, non-classic theatre has been to present on the stage the illusion of ordinary life. The audience looks through a keyhole at the private life of its neighbors. A play is praised for the accuracy of its reporting and photography— "accuracy" here meaning the absence of exaggeration, interpretation or even accent. Sometimes the severity of this formula has been relaxed, and a little democratic good will or Christian sentiment was admitted. I am speaking, as I trust you recognize, of the naturalistic play, still very much with us in the form of what Boris Aronson calls "the play about one's relations." At the time when I was reviewing Broadway plays and saw them all, I was surprised if I ever got to see anything on stage besides the middle-class American home. An American designer only needs one set for his whole repertoire. It consists of an American house, shown inside and out, and possibly upstairs and down. Such is the richness and variety of naturalistic design. What is called in this country The Method in acting is largely devoted to creating on stage the illusion of ordinary behavior. And the word "ordinary" receives a push downward. According to this philosophy, a belch would always seem more real than a song. Such is the richness and variety of naturalistic acting.

But mark this paradox. Although naturalism is the dominant mode of modern drama, all the leading modern dramatists have tried to get away from it. They have one and all tried to get back to that classic theatre in which the figures are larger or smaller than life but never of average size. For the classic theatre does not present the illusion of ordinary life; it presents a vision of life both better and worse than the ordinary. Life is caught at its magnificent and its terrible moments, and so we are taken out of the banal moment in which we find ourselves, caught in a swifter rhythm, a heightened mode of existence. We do not go to the classic theatre in order to recognize the familiar—"just what my uncle George always says"—but to be astonished at revelations of the unsuspected. And though it is a long way from Uncle George's frame house to Macbeth's blasted heath, a classic drama could be set in Uncle George's frame house if the playwright were able to see through the familiar to the unfamiliar, beyond the cliché to the archetype.

There is no important modern dramatist who has not tried to do this, and it is surprising how many of them, in their search for the classic, have hit upon the classical in its historical sense—the Greek. What is attempted in *Mourning Becomes Electra* is not, it seems to me, entirely achieved, but the nature of the attempt is clear and right. It is an attempt to remove the clutter of naturalistic irrelevance and get down to a classic base. In order to arrive at a classic drama of American life, O'Neill used a classical Greek story. In that instance, I believe, the Greek cargo was too heavy for the ship, and the vessel sank, yet it sank nobly, with all on board singing an older and finer song than Nearer, my God, to Thee.

A more recent case is Arthur Miller's *A View from the Bridge*. The play was improved by the removal of explicitly Greek elements. Greece remains the inspiration of the play or, rather, Greece is what helped Mr. Miller several steps along the road from naturalism to classic drama.

Even the so-called "masterpieces of naturalism" turn out, when looked at more closely, to be departures from naturalism. Take Strindberg's *The Father,* a play usually assigned an important part in the naturalistic movement. The fact is that Strindberg had been pondering the *Oresteia* of Aeschylus, and had come across the theory that it reflects the struggles leading to the creation of the patriarchal family. In *The Father* he had in mind the break-up of the patriarchal family and the threatened return of matriarchy. He thought of *The Father* as his *Agamemnon.* Here is another play that is not only classic but classical.

Even the man who made the word Naturalism heard all over the world—Emile Zola—did not champion the tame version of it that has been its main manifestation, nor did he let his own theories limit his creative writing. It was his pleasure to invoke science. Nonetheless, when he uses the idea of heredity, we are less close to any scientific genetics than we are to Moira, the Greek Fate. From Zola's hereditary criminal of *La Bête Humaine* it is only a step to hereditary disease as treated by Ibsen in his *Ghosts;* for although critics bred in the naturalistic tradition continue to speak of syphilis as the subject of this play, and some even add that the play is obsolete now that syphilis can be cured, the real subject is the curse on the house of Alving. It is not accidental that, in approaching a Sophoclean subject, Ibsen resorts to Sophoclean technique: the truth is forced out in a swift series of catastrophic discoveries.

In comedy there is a similar story to tell. Our only great modern master of comedy, Bernard Shaw, always described himself as an old-fashioned playwright, explaining that he went back over the heads of his contemporaries to Dickens, Fielding, Molière, the commedia dell'arte for his methods. Though he belonged to the same generation as Stanislavsky, and had in his friend and colleague Granville Barker a champion of naturalistic staging, he himself reserved his praises for what he called the classical actor. And he maintained that only classical actors could do his plays, because he had revived in them so many features of the classic theatre, and notably the tirade or long set speech which the actor has to articulate for us with the cool clarity of a musician performing a Bach suite.

By about 1920 the permanent crisis of the modern theatre reached a new stage. What Ibsen had done to the naturalistic theatre might be called boring from within. He had accepted its conventions and its stage. The generation of 1920 refused these concessions. The work of Cocteau, Brecht, Meyerhold meant the rejection of the established type of theatre altogether. A new start was proposed. From zero, one is sometimes told. Yet no movement ever goes back *that* far, because—as I was saying—no artist draws solely on his own experience: he always asks some support from tradition. And when one tradition lets him down, or he chooses to reject a tradition, he does not—whatever he may say—operate without tradition. He falls back on some other tradition. Even painters who have rejected all Western history end up, not as "original" in the sense which the man in the street gives to the word, but as neo-African and the like. Rejection of tradition usually implies nothing more than the rejection of recent traditions in favor of earlier ones. In the more interesting drama of the Twenties we find that, while the naturalistic approach of the immediate past is tabu, every other avenue is open. Brecht explored the Spaniards of the golden age, the English Elizabethans, even the Oriental theatre. It was again a search for the classic in dramatic art, and again the Greek note was the one most often struck. I've mentioned O'Neill. I'm thinking also of Cocteau's *Antigone* and *Orpheus*.

With all this goes a technical change that some people think the most important change of all. The dramatists are no longer writing for a box set hidden behind a proscenium arch. The proscenium arch may still be there, because the buildings can't be made over in a hurry, but it is ignored, canceled out, defied. The box set has been carted off stage forever. What the new generation clamors for is some sort of open stage, possibly Elizabethan, possibly also a Roman circus or a Greek arena. Whether such a physical change is the most important change or not, it is one that implies the others. The different shape and functioning of such a stage implies a fundamentally different technique of drama and, with that, a different view of art and life. Take one feature alone, the relation of the action to the eye of the spectator. In the nineteenth-century theatre, the spectator is asked to peep through a little door, like Alice, into an illuminated garden; in the twentieth-century theatre, the actors are brought out to him. In the one, the spectator is a voyeur; in the other, the actor is an exhibitionist. Here too, in the demands they make on the physique of the stage, the more alert modern playwrights have been searching for the classic theatre. The naturalistic theatre offered a peep through the keyhole into the room across the way. The classic theatre provides a parade ground for passions and thoughts and for the human beings above or below life size who experience them.

Since this is what has been going on, you would, from the artistic point of view, be wasting your time to write the kind of play that one generally sees on Broadway. If you have talent, you should join that pursuit of the classic theatre which is, paradoxically, the search for a truly modern theatre. A great future will be born, if at all, from the fruitful union of our present with such a past.

What do you want, actually? It's your wishes that carry the weight. Not what you tell your friends are your wishes. Not what you sometimes think are your wishes. Not what you habitually assume are your wishes. But what you finally find to be your wishes. Your real wishes.

Emerson warned us against wishing, really wishing, for things—because one is likely to get them. If your real wish is to become a prostitute, you will become one; in the theatre, it will be quite easy; and you will never live to regret it; even your old age will be provided for in articles you can write on What Made Me What I Am Today. Your letter to me suggests, rather, that you wish to be a dramatist. If you do, you will have to try it and find out. Time will show if you really are one. Meanwhile, see yourself as a writer and, by consequence, an artist.

Even if you *are* a dramatist, you may not "succeed." That will hurt your feelings very much, especially when you see your non-dramatist friend becoming The Successful Dramatist. An artist wants success. He does not, however, insist on it. His failure to insist on it, though a source of glee among those who exploit him, stems from strength in the artist himself: success is something he can do without, if with difficulty. His pride clamors for satisfaction even more than his vanity; he is a serious chap; he will buy lasting reputation even at the price of immediate fame.

As for you, young sir, if you find you are not a dramatist, and Broadway agrees with you, you will try something else willy-nilly; if there are agonies, they will not be agonies of choice. If you find you are not a dramatist, but Broadway finds you *are* one, the inducement will be considerable to change your mind and become convinced of what you know is not true—a common type of conviction nowadays, and one which is the tie that binds the two most famous streets in America: Broadway and Madison Avenue.

If you find you are a dramatist, and Broadway agrees, try to *stay* a dramatist; it will not be easy. If you find you are a dramatist, and Broadway doesn't agree, that will not be easy either; but you *will* stay a dramatist; you won't be able to help it.

Can playwriting be taught? You have just been the would-be playwright and I have been the would-be teacher. Have you learned anything? Not anything, certainly, that comes between the rise and fall of the curtain. We have stood all this time outside the theatre wondering whether to go in, and I have said: "Do you wish to enter? Then enter—tentatively. Do you have talent? When you know, decide whether to stay." Which is all very preliminary. But then, you aren't yet twenty. And I have met "students of playwriting." Their average age seems to me to be about ninety and probably is in fact over twenty-five. Few of them have explored their wishes (or notable lack of wishes), their talent (or truly remarkable lack of talent). So perhaps they missed that first lesson, which had for theme: To WRIGHT OR NOT TO WRIGHT? You have just had it. Sincerely yours,

Eric Bentley

(1960)

THE THEATRE OF
COMMITMENT

A RECENT LITERARY CONFERENCE announced its
topic as Commitment or Alienation. I take this to
mean that the public relations men believe, first,
that these words are the great eye-catchers of the
moment and, second, that they represent alternative ways of life for artists today. The Committed
artist is one who is publicly protesting against
American policy in Vietnam; the Alienated artist
is one who is sitting the war out and waiting for
Godot in sulky solitude. Artists who are following
any other line of action or inaction simply aren't
"with it."

I start with public relations because that and
not the garden of Eden is where things nowadays
do start. Also, public relations sheds its aura of
unreality on the whole topic, and it is hard to get
at the reality without first dispelling the aura. Fur-

ther, public relations has its own dialectic. Beginning by flattering a subject, lending it importance by means of a glamorous terminology, it ends by throwing suspicion on it, and all persons connected with it. Take the observation I have just made that—once we have uttered the words Commitment and Alienation—artists following any other line of action or inaction would not be considered "with it." This means that, once these words are published, with capital initials, they impel artists to declare themselves Committed or Alienated lest they find themselves in outer darkness. To say this is to impugn the motives of all the committed and all the alienated: nothing is involved, it is suggested, but the desire to be in the swim.

Naturally, in any social movement, there is much mere fashion-following. "I will join if you will, and you will join if the neighbors are joining or if those you look up to think it chic to join." But this situation is not what I am calling attention to. I am calling attention to the way the situation is now exploited by the publicity racket. They need labels to attract attention. They intend a compliment by using them. But the final result is an insult to the thing labeled.

It makes no difference, by the way, that the public relations men are often employees of colleges and universities. And of course it is often the case that they don't regard themselves as public relations men. Their official titles may be President, Dean or plain Professor.

Take symposia on TV, especially so-called educational TV. It all begins with the commendable desire to get the best men, and the modish topic is assumed to be what will attract them, not to mention the public. Commitment. Alienation. Theatre of the Absurd. Theatre of Cruelty. Half a dozen celebrities are brought before the cameras. An academic public relations man mediates between them and the attendant masses. Much smiling. Not much thinking. The millions have heard of theatre of cruelty, and it is concluded that there is a Cultural Explosion. (What an apt expression the phrase Cultural Explosion is—suggesting as it does some cultural equivalent of Hiroshima and Nagasaki.) The trick is this: the public is to think the half dozen celebrities were brought before the cameras for some lofty, cultural reason; if no such reason is apparent, that is because culture is a mysterious business. Actually, the purpose of the whole thing was merely to bring half a dozen celebrities before the cameras. In educational TV, that is a self-justifying act. And on commercial TV it is justified, if not by itself, then by the increased audience for the commercials.

I have accepted the word Commitment for my title because I am not willing to have it relegated to TV symposia and Sunday supplements; because, in short, I think more than a mere fashion is involved. Behind the current discussion of Commitment is the perennial discussion as to whether art should teach or give pleasure. Of that discussion I would only observe here that it is full of paradoxes, and inevitably so, since to be taught can itself be a pleasure, while, conversely, to be given a pleasure may also be to be taught something. Over the course of Western history, the didactic view of art has predominated. Aristotle took the view that the purpose of poetry is pleasure but, on the other hand, he divided pleasures into higher and lower; and one man's higher pleasure is another man's edification. Also, Aristotle said that the most pleasurable thing of all was the learning process.

Perhaps the relevant question for us is why this subject has become urgent again in the past hundred years. For this period has produced not only the doctrine of Commitment but the theory which stands at the opposite pole—the name was not Alienation originally, but Estheticism, Art for Art's Sake. The idea was to keep art pure from the world's vulgarity, and that vulgarity was seen as covering a great deal of territory. The pure artist is not a philistine, nor a politician, he is not even a man of ideas. Instead, he "walks down Piccadilly/ With a poppy or a lily/ In his transcendental hand." The pre-Raphaelite image of the artist became dated long ago, but just the other day a British poet protested against all the Commitment in modern England with the remark that he thought poets should be nightingales, and one of the great efforts at tragedy in twentieth-century drama—Hofmannsthal's *The Tower*—has as its subject the losing fight which in our time the artist puts up to preserve his human purity. Wallace Stevens said: "In the conflict between the poet and the politician the chief honor the poet can hope for is that of remaining himself." So strong was Mr. Stevens' commitment to non-Commitment.

Wallace Stevens' words could be taken another way. Everything depends on time and place. Suppose we heard that the two Soviet writers who recently went to jail had said: "In the conflict between the poet and the politician the chief honor the poet can hope for is that of remaining himself"? We would then find the pronouncement utterly political and conclude that the speakers were committed to liberalism. Similarly, what some consider the estheticism of Pasternak was an active anti-Stalinism. We have grown used to conceding that silence is an act, and an act of cowardice, when speaking out in protest might do some good. We have to concede also that silence is an act, and an act of courage, when speaking out in conformity and flattery is expected of one. The "esthetic" Pasternak withdrew into his "ivory tower"; was silent for a long time; then came out with highly "esthetic" poetry and fiction. This sequence indicates a Commitment, a protest against politics that itself implies a politics.

It was not only with the generation of Stevens and Pasternak that estheticism came to be a form of Commitment. We see something parallel in the life and creed of Oscar Wilde. Wilde said art was perfectly useless. He meant that he didn't want art reduced to the role of little moralistic mottos on Auntie's mantelpiece. He was attacking the exploitation of art by a narrow and philistine utilitarianism. He actually considered art the most useful thing in existence, so far as the good life and the making of a good world are concerned. Only, since art itself provides an image of the good life, and the world an image of the bad life, he wanted the world to learn to be useful to art, not art to be useful to the world. He was the most committed of men. He not only preached anarchistic socialism; his parading of the esthetic way of life was his form of direct action. As an anarchist he refused to leave the changing of the world to history and to movements and insisted on creating a small new world wherever he personally trod.

Am I arriving at the conclusion that all artists are committed? Well, all serious authors are; but that is not what is meant when we speak today of Commitment with a capital C. We mean a political Commitment. And we do not only mean that an artist has political views; we mean that his political views enter into his art.

Translators of Sartre have been explaining that the French word "engagement," which they render as Commitment, has two implications: first, that one is involved in politics willy-nilly; second, that one voluntarily accepts the consequences of a particular political stand. Uncommitted writers are those who don't concede the willy-nilly involvement or who don't concede that it makes any difference. They also are apt to reject a particular political stand on the grounds of its unpleasant attendant circumstances. By declaring allegiance —the Uncommitted are quick to complain—you make yourself an accomplice of the crimes and errors of your leaders and associates. Committed authors retort that the Uncommitted are accomplices of the crimes and errors of whatever leaders they have merely acquiesced in. Inaction is also a moral posture. Being in the world at all entails complicity. The Uncommitted consider themselves innocent because they have not done certain things. That their abstention from these actions may have had terrible consequences is something they *won't* consider. That their non-abstention may have been indispensable if the good was to result is something else they won't consider. The Committed say with Sartre in his letter to Camus

> . . . to deserve the right to influence men who struggle it is first of all necessary to take part in their struggle; it is first of all necessary to accept many things if one wishes to try to change several of them.

Sartre's play *Dirty Hands* is the classic presentation of this point. Its main message, surely, is that we have to be willing to get our hands dirty; that is, bloody.

Is the literature of Commitment by definition on one political side rather than another?

That is a historical question, and speaking historically one would have to answer it in the positive. Relative to the general social situation, the literature of Commitment is radical. It is a literature of protest, not approval, of outrage, not tribute. This proposition is only reinforced by the fate of attempts to disprove it in practice. There was a Jesuit play written to defend Pius XII against Hochhuth's *The Deputy*. That is a doomed kind of project, whatever the talent of the author, because the roots of the Hochhuth play are in a sense of outrage pre-existing in the playwright and other people. Saying they shouldn't be outraged is beside the dramatic point. If the counter-playwright should succeed in presenting a Pius who is not outrageous he will thereby be producing a play that is not dramatic.

You could have a viable play against J. Edgar Hoover, but not one in favor of him. The Commitment of literature could easily be to Robin Hood, less easily to the Sheriff of Nottingham.

Again, you can be for Goliath against David. In politics, today, that is called being pro-American. But Goliath cannot find a literature of Commitment to back him; David always could—only in fact from that literature do we know his story. Poor Goliath!

In the nineteen thirties, the Commitment of many writers was to anti-Hitler literature. It is true that certain writers supported Hitler, and that some of them attempted to produce a literature of Commitment in support of the Führer, but they got nowhere, for essentially what Hitler wanted was sycophancy. Failing that, he would settle for . . . Art for Art's Sake.

Take the theatre. After 1933 the radical German authors couldn't be performed any more. But this did not mean that the theatres were flooded with Nazi plays. There weren't enough Nazi plays to make a trickle, let alone a flood. The German theatre chiefly stages classics, and continued to do so in the Nazi period. The classics had suddenly become all the more necessary. And so the Nazi regime cherished the classics, at any rate when the classics had no offence in them—that is, when they were pure; that is, when they were apolitical. So Art for Art's Sake had a second lease on life—with, of course, a second, somewhat revised significance.

It would seem that Art for Art's Sake is very often what the Attorney General's office calls a *front* for other activities. In Oscar Wilde's case, it was, if you insist, a front for anarchism. In the case of the Germans of a generation ago, it was a front for Nazism and made a special appeal to the German cultured philistine who likes his art noble, archaic and re-assuring. Such was the "reaction-formation" following upon a great era of uncomfortable modernism. It is remarkable but, in that era, going to a Mozart concert could be a gesture directed against the "Jewish conspiracy in world music" (that is, Schoenberg or, if you prefer, Kurt Weill).

What about Alienation? It is not my subject, but if it can be journalistically touted as the opposite pole from Commitment, it may have some place in a discussion of the latter that would like to be dialectical or at any rate not one-sided. The term was taken by Marx from Hegel, and applied to the divorce of the laborer from the fruits, and from the significance, of his labor. From there it has declined—in recent years rather sharply—into signifying merely the younger generation's feeling that it has been left out of things by its parents and teachers. That the term Alienation popularly has this rather unsubtle meaning only makes it the more surprising that Commitment should be popularly regarded as its opposite. When there is a relationship between the two, it is surely not of opposition at all but directly temporal and causal: *after* being Alienated, and *because* one is Alienated, one the more readily Commits oneself. I am, of course, thinking now of the American youth who passes from merely negative revulsion against parents and teachers into espousal of a cause. But that is such a simple and old and well-known sequence that the big words, ponderously if lovingly translated from the revered German and French respectively, are not needed to describe it.

Do the terms Commitment and Alienation serve to describe the two current ways of writing drama? At any rate, if someone said they did, one would know what plays were being referred to. The Committed playwrights are Brecht, Sartre, the social playwrights of modern England, such as John Osborne, and the new generation of German playwrights, such as Rolf Hochhuth, Peter Weiss and Martin Walser. The Alienated playwrights are those otherwise coming under the rubric Theatre of the Absurd: Beckett, Ionesco, Genet. Peter Weiss's *Marat/Sade* might even be seen as a battleground on which the armies of Commitment and Alienation fight it out. In which case, was Peter Weiss himself Committed or Alienated when he wrote that play? There has been fierce debate on the point, and this again makes me wonder if the terms must be used antithetically. No doubt not all persons seen as Alienated must also be seen as Committed? If a Commitment, as I have suggested, properly implies a radical protest, then it is not likely to be made except by those who have already made a radical break. And what we call making a radical break could also be seen as a process of recognizing that a break has already occurred: one was alienated, one was repulsed and rejected, and, knowing it, one rose up, a rebel against the alienators, against the alienating society. I am now trying to give the words back a little legitimate dignity so that they might again refer to something more than adolescent tantrums and sulks.

The alienation Marx spoke of is reflected in the literature of the epoch he spoke of and the epochs that have followed. That is well known. Nonetheless, pure alienation would not produce art at all. The absolutely alienated worker is a desolate, a spiritually annihilated creature. He can only either languish and die or let rage give him back a portion of his humanity and rise in revolt. After the revolt, alienation will be ended in this world; and even before the revolt, it has been mitigated, rendered less complete, by revolt itself. Literature, for its part, may express and dramatize alienation in images unutterably blank and painful, yet it is exposed to the paradox that the act of doing this is not itself blank and painful. The writer takes pleasure in expressing alienation, and his audience takes pleasure in responding to the expression. Any "literature of alienation" is therefore a partial conquest of alienation, just like the fighting worker's efforts on the barricades.

In Samuel Beckett, the positive, or non-alienated, element is not limited to factors one could isolate as purely technical or purely esthetic. His work also has features which show moral conviction and, secondly, revolt. Godot may not be coming, but that does not diminish our moral approval of the two tramps who kept their appointment. The philosophy is firmly stoical, and the humor of the whole proceeding suggests cool defiance.

Is this to say that Beckett is not Alienated but Committed? Not under the definition I am using, which insists on political Commitment. But could not *Waiting for Godot* be political theatre all the same? When Jan Kott was asked: What is the place of Bertolt Brecht in the Polish theatre? he answered: "We do Brecht when we want Fantasy. When we want sheer Realism, we do *Waiting for Godot*." The most apolitical of writers—as we have already seen—can become political in given political circumstances. To be apolitical may indeed be to take a political stand, just as—notably in Poland—to be religious may be to take a political stand. And so it has been the paradoxical destiny of *Godot* to express the "waiting" of the prisoners of Auschwitz; as also the prisoners behind the walls and barbed wire of Walter Ulbricht; as also the prisoners behind the spiritual walls and barbed wire of totalitarian society generally; as also the prisoners behind the spiritual walls and barbed wire of societies nearer home. And there is no doubt a lesson in the fact that these things had not really ever been expressed in works that tried to express them more directly. As A. Alvarez has written in *Commentary:*

The real destructive nihilism acted out in the extermination camps was expressed artistically only in works like Beckett's *Endgame* or *Waiting for Godot,* in which the naked, unaccommodated man is reduced to the role of helpless, hopeless, impotent comic, who talks and talks and talks in order to postpone for a while the silence of his own desolation.

But this is to put it too negatively. Estragon and Vladimir do not only wait. *In* waiting—the original title is *"En* attendant Godot"—they show human dignity. They have kept their appointment, even if Godot has not kept his. A lot of comment on Beckett has gone wrong in taking for granted that Godot will not come, but hope does spring eternal, and even Auschwitz prisoners hoped to get out. In this element of hope lies the politics of the play. Without it, *Godot* would be anti-political, inviting its audience to lose itself in complete despair or to seek redemption from despair outside the world depicted (presumably in the other world of religion).

Many a play acquires urgency through special circumstances, and one should think of political drama less in terms of the script alone than in terms of when and where it is presented, not to mention how.

What I have said up to now is essentially about literature in general, or about drama as literature,

but there exists a drama of Commitment which is
not just another instance of literature of Commitment. It is *theatre,* and puts its message across in a
special way, a way that is perhaps especially suita-
ble to the purposes of a Committed author. It also
differs from other forms of drama, and especially
from the traditional patterns of tragedy and comedy. Let me again—and this time at some
length—cite *The Deputy.*

A priest was quoted in the press as saying that it
would all have mattered so little if only *The Deputy* had not been a play. This comment suggests,
more than anything one is likely to read in
dramatic criticism, that a play can somehow both
focus and enlarge discontent. Books have been
written on Catholicism and the Nazis, some of
them with a viewpoint similar to Hochhuth's, and
one more such book would make little difference.
The Deputy made a big difference, so we are au-
thoritatively informed, *because it is a play.* A
play—this is the first meaning we derive from the
statement—is by definition a "dramatization": it
brings out what is memorable and striking in the
material, possibly to the point of sensationalism.
Dramaturgy implies a whole armory of devices for
bringing order out of the chaos of facts and fic-
tions. Greater intelligibility reinforces greater vi-
vidness. The unmanageable becomes manageable,

even as the blurred becomes the clear. It is not hard to see what interested parties have to fear. If they have a bad conscience, they have to fear the *dies irae* when the truth will suddenly out and the malefactors will be punished. They have to fear the hard outline which a play can draw around the truth; they have to fear the power of conviction a play can carry. If they have a good conscience they have to fear what they will see as the specious plausibility of the drama. Pirandello has it that life, because it is fact, need not be plausible, but that art, because it is fiction, has plausibility as its sine qua non. How terrible, then, the plausibility of a fiction which poses as fact! Pirandello used to notice how much more cogent were his mad wife's fantasies than his own recollection of the truth. How ruefully those who consider *The Deputy* a mad fantasy of Hochhuth's must think of their own unavailing efforts to counter the play with *their* recollection of the truth! They cannot but consider Hochhuth's recourse to the dramatic form as in itself a trick.

Luckily for their peace of mind, such persons all seem to have found *The Deputy* quite a bad play. Consequently, though they must resent the fact that Hochhuth resorted to the dramatic form at all, they cannot but rejoice that (as they see it) he failed to exploit that form for anything like what it is worth. Yet even this is cold comfort, since, in the first place, the dramatic form has a special impressiveness even when handled with only moderate skill and, secondly, more importantly, since it is not just a form of writing that is in question but a particularly potent form of presentation: enactment before an audience. Here again, one may have a low opinion of the particular manifestation: one may fault the actors, the directors and even the audience. But here again there are forces which remain operative when actors, director and audience leave much to be desired. Theatre is sur-real. The little ritual of performance, given just a modicum of competence, can lend to the events represented another dimension, a more urgent reality. And, to the actual, present force of the enactment for the spectators who are there, one must add its symbolic force for those who hear about it. Putting Pius XII on stage at all is a highly charged act; and, so far from being illegitimate, a feeling of shock that he *was* put on stage is part of the game, and was on the cards from the beginning.

The Puritans were always right in their apprehensions, whatever one thinks of their ethics, and it was with their usual well-grounded fear that they always tried to stop this or that from being represented on a public stage. And the Puritans' anti-type, Queen Cleopatra, agrees with them that the worst way of being exhibited for disapproval would be to be exhibited on a public stage. Once again, the feeling arises that a swindle is involved. On stage, falsehood is not merely uttered, it seems to become truth. You see Pius XII in three dimensions *actually* doing those dreadful things which, *actually*—but this second *actually* is weaker than the first—he did not do.

To the fear of the theatrical occasion add fear of the theatre as an institution. Again, those who feel the fear do know what they are afraid of. A churchman readily understands the power of the theatre because it is a power that resembles his own. Putting it brutally, both church and theatre lend themselves to demagogy. Each one at its best tries to inspire and edify but, when not at its best, is content to seduce and degrade. Men on a stage, like men in a pulpit, have their histrionic opportunities maximized, while those in the plush seats or wooden pews are placed in a position of maximum vulnerability. A maximum of eloquence and magic from those in charge, with an audience or congregation that is not allowed to answer back! Neither church nor theatre has evolved in an atmosphere of rationality, let alone of give and take.

What must be especially galling to the church-

man today is that the stage sometimes has the edge
over the pulpit. For one thing, the modern theatre
audience is not limited to a particular congregation, but is general. It, and not the church, is
truly catholic. There had been criticism of Pius
XII among the Faithful, but the news had scarcely
spread *beyond* the Faithful. Hochhuth was more
dangerous because of his general audience, as Cardinal Spellman acknowledged in his devious way
when accusing the playwright of stirring up strife
between Christian and Jew. No doubt there are
advantages in the church's holiness, real or assumed, but, where criticism is concerned, the
greater advantage lies with harsh secularity. That
the theatre may have its origin in religion, and has
sometimes kept company with religion, should not
prevent us from seeing how thoroughly secular an
institution it still is and how inclined it is to take
full advantage of its secularity. Thus the theatre takes Pius XII out of the dim candlelight of the
church and turns its spotlights on him. He may
never recover. Naturally, those who revered him
were offended: it was their reverence that had kept
him in twilight. Of course there is fearful vulgarity
in a Pope's becoming a topic of chit-chat at Sardi's
and the Algonquin, but from Hochhuth's standpoint that is the price to be paid for the right to
discuss Pius with eyes no longer closed in prayer,

in tones no longer hushed by awe. There is no need for a theatre of cruelty, for theatre is itself cruel. . . .

If only *The Deputy* had not been a play! That is one of the two most pointed things that can be said about it. The other is: but is *The Deputy* really a play?

People putting this second question have generally had in mind that *The Deputy* is inordinately documentary. Hochhuth has unloaded bucketfuls of factual reports, and actual quotations, into his dialogue. That, we say, is not drama, but history. However, our saying so turns out to be a criticism only of particular passages. The fault which people find in the play as a whole is that it is not historical enough. They find it, on the contrary, too melodramatic. They complain that this is a stage villain of a Pope, whereas the actual Pius XII had pleasingly human traits that are not shown in the play. Actually, then, their complaint is not that *The Deputy* is not a play, but that it is only a melodramatic play.

Since evidently what is being called for is an unmelodramatic *Deputy*, we are entitled to ask what such a work would be like. Presumably it would be a play in which Pius' bad traits were balanced by good traits. The laws of dramatic structure would then bring it about that Pius's antagonist, Father Fontana, would also have his good traits balanced by bad ones. At least one critic actually observed of *The Deputy* that Bernard Shaw would have given the Pope a case. Now a "case" implies a good deal more than some pleasant character traits. A man might be pleasant, or even good, and still not have a "case" in the historical situation described. So, to characters of mixed good and evil, we must add—in this prescription for a *Deputy* which is a "real play"—a *theme* of mixed good and evil, a *problem* in which there is a case for both sides.

In making these technical changes in the play we would change its philosophy and remove its *raison d'être.* No affront would have been offered to Pius XII. Faults, in a context of non-faults, only make a man the more human, and so the more amiable. If in his turn the good Father Fontana has some notable faults, the score is evened up, and Hochhuth's play has been made over into something completely innocuous, proving only what would be conceded in advance, and enunciating the world-shaking principle that none of us is perfect.

And yet the theory of drama behind the criticism of Hochhuth is a well-proven one. It is true that *Saint Joan* (for example) becomes a better play because of the weight Shaw gives to the Other

Side. *Saint Joan* does show a conflict of right with right, and a fascinating kind of conflict it is, and one which the art of drama is well suited to present.

In a sense, the play Hochhuth's critics wanted him to write had already and triumphantly been written. It is Schiller's *Don Carlos.* On the face of it, Philip is the villainous tyrant, Posa, the virtuous rebel. But Schiller then does just what, as students of the drama, we may wish him to do: he gives Philip a kind of rightness and some endearing personal traits, while he offsets the more obvious rightness of Posa's arguments with a personal arrogance which can only horrify us. Indeed, the play is in the end more damaging to Posa than to Philip, and it could be that critics of Hochhuth who have limited their demands to more sympathy for Pius really wanted no sympathy at all for Father Fontana.

I have implied that if *The Deputy* humanized Pius, and stated a case for him, then the play would be affirming something as interesting and significant as the fact that ten minus ten equals zero. But why should this be so? The statement would not apply to *Don Carlos.* There, the humanizing of Philip, and the statement of a case for him, adds to the meaning and to the dramatic tension. What is the difference?

We can get at it, I think, by asking what would happen if *Don Carlos* were re-written on the lines of *The Deputy*. Philip would then be pure tyrant, Posa, pure idealist. Thousands of German readers and spectators have actually taken them this way, and enjoyed the play very much. It disturbed no preconceptions; on the contrary, it made a very reassuring melodrama. Polemically speaking—and we *are* speaking of polemics—Hochhuth's project is very different. He is taking a respected figure, and removing every reason why we should respect him.

Is it fair to remove even objective evidence that there were things about Pius to respect? If this were a biography, it would simply be unfair. But drama is not only more selective than biography, it is selective according to different principles. It never lays claim to an interest in all of a man, but only in that part of him that is manifest in a chosen and partially fabricated Action. A playwright may start with a historical figure, but that does not absolve him from the job of putting him through the mill (or sausage machine, if you insist) of the drama. By all means, if a Shavian drama on Pius XII were planned, then a case for Pius would emerge: Shaw would even invent positive and likable traits for him, as he did for Cauchon, but the net result in a Shavian drama with this subject matter would be to excuse, at least in some measure, what Pius did. Let some Shavian playwright try it: speech is free. Meanwhile, is it not also legitimate to plan a play, not in extenuation of Pius's actions and non-actions, but in condemnation of them?

And is melodrama the best word to describe what happens if we do? I have just said that many Germans have taken *Don Carlos* as melodrama, and have enjoyed it as such. The last clause is essential. To convert material into melodrama is to re-arrange it for our delectation: it must be fun. Is *The Deputy* fun, and should it be? Was Hochhuth's aim a stirring narrative, spiced with a facile appeal to conventional notions of right and wrong? Surely we are not approaching an understanding of his enterprise by this route. Let us try another.

Let us ask: from what realities does Hochhuth start? Clearly, with the realities of the Nazi era and the Nazi regime. Now if he had put Hitler on stage, one can imagine how monstrous the characterization would have been. Consequently some people would have said: "This is very unfair. The Führer actually loved dogs and children. He was nice to Eva Braun. Some of his social policies brought real welfare to thousands of people." A playwright could indeed bring in enough of such items to balance exactly the negative traits. In that way, certain demands could be met. I could argue that, even as truth, a portrait of that man conceived in hatred might be more valid than one written according to the dogma that all men are a blend of good and evil, but my point here is that the aim of a play is not portraiture, and that the choice of such material as this does not arise from the desire merely to state what went on.

It is not likely that a play would be written about Hitler in the first place except to express, not merely disapproval, but outrage. Bernard Shaw did try to represent him in the Shavian vein: the effort (in *Geneva*) has very little value or significance. Charlie Chaplin's effort (in *The Great Dictator*) has more value and significance insofar as Chaplin was outraged, but has limited value and significance in that the outrages of Hitler cannot find adequate expression in the art of Charlie Chaplin. . . .

Two things stand out in our time: first, that gigantic outrages against mankind are constantly being committed and, second, that mankind is not outraged by them. As the outrages themselves increase in scope, our ability to respond to them diminishes. Have we got used to them? Have we grown bored by them? Can we tell ourselves someone invented them, and they didn't really happen?

Were they at least vastly exaggerated? These questions are all active in our little brains and nervous systems, mingling with each other in a fashion logically indefensible but psycho-logically irresistible.

The crassest rationalization of all is that Outrage is a name for what others do to us, and never for what we do to them. A factor Americans haven't understood about German anti-Semitism is that the Germans at the time felt too outraged *by* the Jews to feel outraged *for* them. You will retort that they had no right to feel that way, and I will retort that that is just my point, and applies to the lack of widespread outrage in America over the bombing of Hiroshima. Americans at the time were full of the horrors, real and imaginary, which the Japanese had perpetrated against Americans.

Each country, today, has a bad conscience, and particularly the great powers, but each is very concerned to disown it by the diversionary maneuver of incessant talk about the misdemeanors of others. The others may in each case have much more than a mote in their eye, yet that is no reason for denying the beam in one's own. The politicians are not concerned to cure this disease, they are concerned to exploit it, and so what would like to regard itself as a dialogue between East and West is only a recriminatory harangue. The other side is bad, and responsible for everything that is wrong. Our side (whichever our side is) is good, and even its most hideous actions are necessities imposed by the other fellow's iniquity. If you are looking for melodrama, my friends, don't look in Hochhuth's *The Deputy,* look in your morning newspaper.

Luckily for our sanity, there have been objections, and especially from men of religion and men of thought, from Pope John to Martin Buber, from Martin Luther King to Arnold Toynbee, from Bertrand Russell to Walter Lippmann. And the young people are in eruption. As for artists, Hochhuth can be taken as representative of those among them who see their task at this time to lie in what we may call declarations of conscience. *Of course,* the aim is not to show that Hitler had a human side. The reason for presenting Hitler would be to show that a human being can, to all intents and purposes, become inhuman and monstrous. That is Outrage Number One. And Outrage Number Two is that so many men were not outraged—*are* not outraged. Some worshiped Hitler. Some gave him sneaking respect. Many thought that, well, he wasn't as ineffective as a lot of other people. Some merely accepted him, whether from fear of the alternative, inertia or completely open-minded skepticism.

What Hochhuth believes to have been the attitude of the historical Pius XII entails a particular outrage. Pius was no Nazi: his conscience might have been clearer if he had been. Pius loved reactionary, old Germany, and dreaded more than anything else atheistic, new Russia. Things he would hear about what his Germans were doing would make him nervous, but he would not let himself become their enemy like the Russians. Was he not Christ's Deputy in the war against anti-Christian Communism? So Pius XII left the Jews to their fate. Auschwitz was liberated by his enemies, the Russian atheists.

For Hochhuth, Pius embodies a double offense. Politically, he falls into the trap, or remains in the rut, of imagining that all will be well provided only we are always and exclusively Anti-Communist. Morally, this representative of Jesus turns out to be a Pontius Pilate, washing his hands of the moral issue that faced him. So finally he does not represent Christ but, instead, represents all those in our time who, while refusing open, enthusiastic support to the Monster, give him an acquiescence that is really *carte blanche*. Americans who give *carte blanche* to Presidents to wage unjust wars have no very solid grounds for feeling superior to Pius XII.

I have mentioned that a play was written in Pius' defense, and I have suggested that that kind of thing is doomed to failure, because all that can be brought to Pius' defense is an argument. Anyone who would write a counter-Hochhuth has already made the mistake of assuming that what *The Deputy* presents is an argument against Pius. But the real "offense" of Hochhuth is precisely that he takes for granted that Pius is indefensible and that no argument could make any difference. That is the kind of play *The Deputy* is. Of course, Hochhuth makes assumptions that not all can accept. Of course, his play is not addressed to everybody. Yet, in one sense, it *is* addressed to everybody, for it assumes that right and wrong are known to the human heart, and that if we choose to brush aside all ideology and opinion and current politics, we recognize an outrage when we see it. To make the outrage visible, Hochhuth concentrates upon it, isolates it, shows his Pope Pius as wholly outrageous. And in an unexpected way. Hochhuth by-passes the argument most readily available to him: that Pius was afraid of Hitler. Cowardice would make Pius little, but it would also make him human. This Pius is *in*human in that he is cold, callous, cut off from others, lacking in imagination about them. He cannot feel. He is a non-human human, and, in the circumstances, *of all human types the one least able to represent Jesus Christ.* To the extent that the Hochhuth

portrait is thought of as the historical Pius XII it is
an even more terrible indictment than Catholic
spokesmen have realized.

If *Don Carlos* and *Saint Joan* are precedents, the
prototype is *Antigone*. But for my present purposes
we need to imagine an *Antigone* more primitive
than that of Sophocles, which is, after all, a late
and highly sophisticated reading. Sophocles may
not, as some moderns think, have made Creon as
sympathetic as Antigone herself, but he did offer
him a partial sympathy, and when we do that we
are on the road towards Schiller and Shaw, at the
end of which road stands Anouilh with an Antigone who stands for neuroticism and a Creon
who is a rather sensible chap. With Brecht's Antigone, in which the heroine is wholly right, and
Creon an inhuman tyrant, we are starting out
again where we may presume the story to have
originated in pre-Sophoclean days.

Those who tell us that this spells melodrama
rather than tragedy should not take us aback. We
should, on the contrary, let them spur us on to
look what happens when tragedy is not attempted.
Take the question of how plays end. Tragedy, and
for that matter comedy, farce and melodrama, end
with a suggestion of either pessimism or optimism.
A pessimistic ending tells us that nothing can be
done. An optimistic ending tells us that nothing

need be attempted: since everything is already in order, we should feel reconciled to the All. It is, in fact, hard to put an ending on a play that does not have some such conclusiveness, optimistic or pessimistic. Yet an attempt—often known as the bitter ending—has been made from time to time, and it is bitter because it is not a true ending at all, but is open at the end. We associate it with tragi-comedy, and it has a special point in activist drama, polemical drama, drama of Commitment, because it says: what happens after this is up to you, the public.

A classical instance of such tragi-comedy of Commitment would be Brecht's *Good Woman of Setzuan*. The fortunes of the protagonist go from bad to worse. There can be no comic denouement, but the author will not provide any final cataclysm either. As soon as the main character's position is clearly revealed as an impasse, Brecht refuses to stage a final catastrophe, and, as to denouement, asks the audience to devise one—off stage. Which is only making completely explicit what much bitter, activist tragi-comedy had been doing for generations. (There is a similar explicitness to the end of *The Threepenny Opera*. John Gay had already indicated at the close of his *Beggar's Opera* that what is happening is what happens in Opera, not life. Brecht's version of things is not complete till the audience understands that what happens in life is just the opposite, and that the relation of art and life, here, is that of illusion and reality, false propaganda and fact.)

And at this point, to clear up a possible misunderstanding about Brecht might well be to clear up a misunderstanding about the whole problem of drama and propaganda. The term Propaganda was often applied to Brecht with no other intention than to damage him. It was inevitable, then, that those of us who came to his defense should take either the line that his work was "not propaganda" or the line that it was "more than" propaganda. And I should add that I still think the second of these lines is correct. But polemics, while always needed, always distort the problems, and one way they do so is by luring the polemicist into positions he would never take except in the heat of argument. In this way, those who took Brecht's part were often lured into implying that there is something deplorable about propaganda as such. Hence if Brecht was "more than" propaganda, it could only be "in spite of" propaganda, and even "in contradiction to" the propaganda, not just "in addition" to it.

Brecht the person and Brecht the advocate were not always at one, and some of his plays become more, rather than less, dramatic because the ad-

vocate is outdone by the person. There is a ten
between where Brecht wanted his sympathies
and where they actually were. From this te...
his plays sometimes benefit. In stating this much
we are on firm ground. But the ground is less firm
when we imply that Brecht was well served only by
his unconscious, and is only dramatic unbeknown
to himself and in spite of himself. How much respect can one have for an intellectual playwright
who is so much less aware of what he is doing than
his critics are? And is it fair to offer Brecht the
backhanded compliment implicit in this kind of
criticism without first examining his work in the
terms he himself proposes?

It would surely be fair to question the motives of
the critics as rigorously as they have questioned the
motives of Brecht. I discern a negative motive and
a positive one. The negative one is to discredit the
doctrinal content of Brecht's work, the positive
one is to vindicate him on entirely traditional
lines—and thus make of him essentially a traditional artist working in the principal accepted
genres. Stage directors with this viewpoint present
Brecht as a "classic" bearing witness to the
unchanging human tragedy and comedy. His plays
tend, however, not to get across when presented in
this way, and that surely is a rather conclusive, if
pragmatic, refutation of the viewpoint.

Suppose that, on the other hand, one were to apply to Brecht the theory which Rolf Zimmermann has applied to Hochhuth? Herr Zimmermann maintains [1] that there exists, beside the main traditions of literature, a tradition of polemic. Having its own aim, polemical theatre has its own method. The aim being to recreate the author's sense of outrage, the method is not to use "rounded," "human," equally-right-and-wrong characters, but enactors of the outrageous on the one hand and, on the other, victims of outrage and rebels against outrage. The ending will be the open one of bitter tragi-comedy. A Brecht production infused with this idea does get across to its audience, as has many times been proved. I suggest, then, that it would be wise to take his plays (except for the very early ones) as in the first instance Theatre of Commitment, whatever else they may be as well.

That Brecht's plays are Theatre of Commitment but other things as well has won him approval of a sort from critics who did not share his commitment, but *The Deputy* is Theatre of Commitment and nothing else, and so Hochhuth is open to attack both by those who don't share his convictions and by those who insist on the canons of con-

1. In his essay "Drama or Pamphlet" in my critical anthology *The Storm Over the Deputy.*

ventional drama. His play has been little praised, and yet one cannot believe that it made the impression it did solely because of its subject. The history of literature is strewn with works on big subjects that make no impression at all. It could even be said that the subject of the Nazis had become boring until Hochhuth came along with a play *on* that subject. But if we wish to know if Hochhuth's play is a success we have only to remind ourselves that the purpose of this kind of play is to communicate a sense of outrage. And it *has* communicated a sense of outrage. Is it not Hochhuth's sense of outrage that his opponents are upset by? Surely they didn't get as angry as they did just because they disagreed? The problem, to recapitulate, is that this is, successfully, a play. If only it were a play of ideas, one could handle it by argument. And if it were a play of ideas by Shaw, one could observe what a strong case he had put for Pius. But the author of *The Deputy* is outraged by Pius, and communicates his sense of outrage in a manner that would not seem to brook No for an answer. You have to enter into it, let your heart respond to it—or move out of its path and be outraged *by* it.

To whom does the Theatre of Commitment address itself? Not to everyone. It has human enemies; and human beings who admire the enemies, or enjoy some kind of solidarity with them, cannot but detach themselves and walk out. An enemy does not make a good audience. What about allies? It could be said that they don't need preaching to. Yet propaganda can serve the purposes of ritual, one of which is to confirm people in their convictions and prepare them for renewed struggle. But the ideal audience for the Theatre of Commitment is, I think, neither one set of militants nor the other, but rather a mass of people in the middle, who may be vaguely sympathetic to the cause preached but are a little sluggish and sleepy about it. They may assent but they are not really committed, and the purpose of the Drama of Commitment is not to be *for* Commitment but to get people to commit themselves. Could not most of us say we belong to this audience, and does not the Theatre of Commitment have, by that token, a large enough clientele?

Yet another reason why *The Deputy* is a crucial instance of Commitment is that Hochhuth writes not only for this audience but about it. This is the play about the Nazis that is not about the Nazis but about those who were "a little sluggish and sleepy" in opposing them. The common view is that the leading Nazis bore most of the guilt, a little of which rubbed off on those who went along. Hochhuth would put far more of the guilt on the fellow travelers, and his presentation forces us to realize how much could have been done against the Nazis which was not done. Now a dramatist cannot but present individual cases and in picking his chief individual target Hochhuth made a choice that was perhaps malicious and certainly audacious: the titular head of our soi-disant Christian civilization. But, in Germany, certainly, this Holy Father can easily stand for a lot of other fathers, the fathers of very many of Hochhuth's own generation. This character "is" many middle-aged and elderly Germans of today who claim a spotless record but who can be shown to have been no better than neutral and maybe quite a bit worse. That, though, is only to say that they are "a little sluggish and sleepy," that they are you and I, and that they and we are Hochhuth's audience.

As long as such an audience exists, and urgent reasons exist why they should be roused from their semi-slumber, there is a place for a literature of Commitment, and as long as certain people live in special dread of plays ("Please, God, let it not be a play!"), there is a place for a Theatre of Commitment. Any dent that any theatre can make in the world is no doubt small, but theatre people who on that account give up the effort as hopeless are generally agreeing to make no dent at all. Writing some years ago about T. S. Eliot's wish that *Murder in the Cathedral* might have made inroads on Nazism,* I wrote that this play or any other would have been no use against the SS and the Wehrmacht. There are times when the poet may be called upon to drop the pen and take up, if not the sword, then whatever is the most effective implement of direct action. The years 1942–45 were such times, if such times ever were. And if one were Vietnamese, one might well feel that the Nineteen Sixties were also such a time. In the United States the situation is different indeed. Here the point, surely, is not more violence, but less. Here the point is to subjugate the machine and tame the beast. Here every action and word in the direction of gentleness and restraint is so much to the good. One could say the need was for *civilization,* just that. One could say: *education.* But there is an urgency which neither word suggests, and therefore one must out with it and say: there is a need for *propaganda.*

People tell me that America is so far gone in television, radio and movies, that the poor old stage is as obsolete as the horse and buggy. Obviously that is not true, or our priest could not have been so dismayed to find that *The Deputy* was a play. The idea that the theatre is obsolete

* See page 134 above.

reflects the wish of vested interests that it may become obsolete. The theatre is a threat but would cease to be so were it swamped by the Media. It represents what the powers behind the Media wish to have swamped. It is the last refuge, or one of the last refuges, of personal association, of the simple assembly of persons with common interests at something less huge and overpowering than a stadium. A theatrical event is nothing more than itself: it is not simultaneously seen or heard by the Nation. There is nothing to it but what each person present can see and hear; it is a self-contained human transaction.

Which is not only part of its charm, but part of its value, and is beginning to be felt as such. The young people who are in eruption in America today are not stuck in front of TV sets. It is more often their parents who are to be found in that pitiful posture. The rebellious young have walked out on their parents. They are on the streets outside, playing their guitars. These are years that have even produced a theatre called Theatre in the Street.

There is, of course, nothing wrong with television. When run by human beings for human beings, that invention will be seen to have possibilities. It still won't duplicate the function of theatre. *Theatre is people present:* actors present on stage, spectators present out front, a living contact between the two groups. Everything we call theatre is in that electrico-human circuit, which neither TV nor movies will ever be able to set up. Even when improved, TV will be of the new, mechanized, big-scale world, like Clark Kerr's multiversity. Certainly, theatre is old-fashioned in belonging to the old, intimate, small-scale world. More old-fashioned and also more new-fashioned, because the new generation is defecting in droves from what the middle-aged say is modern and up-to-date. There is no substitute for live human contact. Theatre has the same appeal as coffee houses have proved to have, and in fact, in New York today, there is a more lively theatre in the coffee houses than in the Broadway show shops. As William James made clear, there is something bad about all bigness in human organizations, and the anarchists are certainly on to something when they insist on holding on to the small groups, the personal meetings-together, at all costs. The theatre, accordingly, is an institution for Jamesians and anarchists, and for the Jamesian and anarchist in each of us, to hold on to.

I see that my subject is shifting, here at the close, from Theatre of Commitment to a possible commitment which we might make to theatre. What is the connection between the two themes? A theatre on the street would not necessarily stage *The Deputy*. A coffee house theatre would not necessarily concern itself with Brecht. But there is a degree of "subversion" in the act of theatre itself. Wherever "two or three are gathered," a blow is struck against the abstract non-gatherings of the TV audience as well as against the gatherings of expense-account mobs on Broadway. A blow is struck for the old and obsolete which—if we are lucky (or just persistent?) —shall be the new and modern. Subversiveness, rebellion, revolution in the theatre are not just a matter of program, much less are they to be defined in terms of a particular kind of play.

And as for the particular kind of play I have chiefly been talking about, if it does not have much effect on the world, it may yet have quite a salutary effect on the theatre, always provided that the world consents to go on existing. I make no prophecies. I simply remark that, in the drama of the Nineteen Sixties, the Theatre of Commitment is the principal new presence. There are reasons both political and theatrical to welcome it.

(1966)

NOTES AND
ACKNOWLEDGMENTS

"Is the Drama an Extinct Species?" was commissioned by *The New York Times* during the 1953-4 theatre season for publication in its Sunday Magazine section. When written, however, it was paid for but rejected, like the only other piece I have ever written for this supplement. It was published in the July 1954 issue of *Partisan Review*. "The American Drama 1944–1954" began as a lecture at the Library of Congress, and was first published in the *Avon Book of Modern Writing*, 1954. "What is Theatre?" was first a lecture, presented at the University of Virginia and other institutions; a large part of it then appeared in *The New Republic*. (Of the three essays just mentioned, the first two were reprinted in my book *The Dramatic Event*, 1954, the third in my book *What is Theatre?*, 1956). "Taking Ibsen Personally" has been left in its original form: that of a short ad-

232

dress delivered in the Aula of the University in
Oslo on the occasion of a special "Ibsen Week"
organized to celebrate the fiftieth anniversary of
the playwright's death (1956). It was printed soon
thereafter in the Norwegian periodical *Edda;* the
second part of it appeared in *The Columbia University Forum,* Winter 1957. "The Pro and Con of
Political Theatre" was written during the winter
of 1959–60 as an address delivered at the Carnegie
Institute of Technology, Pittsburgh, and as a paper
submitted to a meeting of the Congress of Cultural
Freedom in Berlin; part of it was then printed in
The Kenyon Review under the title "The Political
Theatre Reconsidered" and part in *The Columbia
University Forum* under the title "The Classic
Theatre in Modern Life." "Letter to a Would-Be
Playwright" began as a talk to the playwrights and
would-be playwrights of the New Dramatists Committee in New York, and was re-written for publication in *Playboy,* December 1960. "The Theatre
of Commitment" was one of the Ullman Memorial
Lectures at Brandeis University, was first printed
in *Commentary,* December 1966, and is here reprinted by special permission of Brandeis University. It will later form part of a volume of Ullman
Lectures. There was some discussion of it in the
columns of *Commentary,* March 1967.

Since all seven essays were written on request, I

may be said to owe the whole book to other people's initiative. For better or for worse, they certainly drew out of me much that I would not otherwise have set down, or perhaps even thought. As there is nothing pleasanter for a human being than to feel wanted, so there is nothing pleasanter for a performer than a command performance. Just to know that someone is interested, just to know that one has an eager audience, however small or special, is reassuring at all times and, in times of unusual stress, a necessity for survival.

E. B.

SPRING *1967*

Thanks are due Mark Minton for making the index and Violet Serwin for typing the manuscript.

INDEX

Abie's Irish Rose, 88, 165
Achard, Marcel, 9
Adams, J. Donald, 79
Aeschylus, 14, 63, 64, 183
Agamemnon, 183
All My Sons, 28, 35
Alvarez, A., 203
Ancient Art and Ritual, 70
Anderson, Judith, 43
Anderson, Robert, 30
Anouilh, Jean, 9, 52, 220
Antigone (of Anouilh), 220
Antigone (of Brecht), 220
Antigone (of Cocteau), 185
Antigone (of Sophocles), 220
Archer, William, 41, 44, 84
Aristophanes, 12, 63, 64
Aristotle, 62, 64, 71, 72, 74, 85, 88
Aristotle's Theory of Poetry and Fine Art, 71
Arms and the Man, 88
Arnold, Matthew, 141
Aronson, Boris, 180
As You Like It, 65
Atkinson, Brooks, 20, 33, 165
Austen, Jane, 75
Autumn Garden, The, 34

Bach, J. S., 97

Balzac, Honoré de, 178
Barker, Granville, 184
Bat, The, 88
Beckett, Samuel, 157, 190, 201, 202–203, 204
Beethoven, Ludwig van, 137, 147
Beggar's Opera, The, 180, 221
Benthall, Michael, 103
Bentley, Eric, xi, 95, 224
Bérard, Christian, 28
Bernstein, Leonard, 142
Bête Humaine, La, 183
Birds, The, 63
Booth, Shirley, 60
Born Yesterday, 32
Bowles, Jane, 40, 43
Brand, 108, 112, 118
Braun, Eva, 214
Brecht, Bertolt, 4, 94–96, 106, 115, 116, 121–122, 127–129, 132–134, 154, 155, 156, 157, 179, 180, 184, 185, 200, 203, 220, 221–224, 231
Brooke, Eleanor, 33
Brothers Karamazov, The, 73
Brown, John Mason, 33
Browning, Robert, 73

Index

Buber, Martin, 217
Bukharin, Nikolai I., 106
Bundy, McGeorge, xii
Butcher, S. H., 71

Caine Mutiny Court Martial, The, 40, 51
Calderon de la Barca, 98
Camino Real, 18
Camus, Albert, 157, 197
Carlyle, Thomas, 63, 83
Catiline, 112, 118
Cenci, The, 72
Chairs, The, 157
Chamberlain, Neville, 110
Chaplin, Charlie, 4, 91, 215
Chayefsky, Paddy, 80–81, 82
Chekhov, Anton, 41, 42, 43, 169, 170
Cherry Orchard, The, 41, 42
Children's Hour, The, 39–40
Chute, Marchette, 82
Clarke-Smith, D. A., 101
Claudel, Paul, 9, 150
Cleopatra, Queen, 208
Clurman, Harold, 26, 27
Cocktail Party, The, 9
Cocteau, Jean, 9, 184, 185
Condon, Richard, 33
Conrad, Joseph, 74, 75, 76
Country Girl, The, 34
Crime and Punishment, 100–101
Crouse, Russel, 18, 33
Crucible, The, 34, 36–40, 51

Dante, 90, 125
Darkness at Noon, 34, 35, 40

Davis, Luther, 18, 31
Death of a Salesman, 28, 30, 34, 35, 144, 145
DeFilippo, Eduardo, 4
Dekker, Thomas, 5
Deputy, The, 197, 205–220, 224–227, 228, 231
Dial M for Murder, 7
Dickens, Charles, 75, 174, 184
Dirty Hands, 197
Divine Comedy, The, 125
Doll's House, The, 99, 112
Don Carlos, 79, 212, 213, 214, 220
Don Juan in Hell (Man and Superman), 86, 129–130
Dostoyevsky, Fyodor, 73, 75, 100–101
Drake, Alfred, 31
Dramatic Event, The, 95
Druten, John van, 40–44
Dryden, John, 69–70
Dumas fils, Alexandre, 89
Dürrenmatt, Friedrich, 154, 155
Duse, Eleonora, 100

Eckermann, J. P., 179
Egmont, 176
Einstein, Albert, 122
Eisenhower, Dwight D., 15
Eisenstein, Sergei, 123
Eisler, Gerhard, 106
Eliot, T. S., 9, 32, 134, 228
Elizabeth I, Queen, 11
Emerson, Ralph Waldo, 187
Emperor and Galilean, 112

End as a Man, 40
Endgame, 204
Enemy of the People, An,
 114, 115, 118
Engels, Friedrich, 107

Father, The, 183
Faubus, Orville, 120–121
Faust (of Goethe) , 176
Fielding, Henry, 184
Fifth Season, The, 20, 21
Fischer, Ruth, 106
*Freedom and the Tragic
 Life*, 75
Freud, Sigmund, 171
Fuchs, Klaus, 137

Galileo, 122
Galileo, 95, 133
Gay, John, 180, 221
Genet, Jean, 201
Ghosts, 91, 100, 102–103,
 108-109, 112, 113, 118,
 183–184
Gibson, William, 144
Gide, André, 112
Glass, Menagerie, The, 11, 44
Goebbels, (Paul) Joseph,
 10, 45, 48
Goethe, Johann Wolfgang
 von, 168, 176, 179
Goldoni, Carlo, 12
Goldwyn, Samuel, 85
*Good Woman of Setzuan,
 The*, 133, 221
Gorki, Maxim, 40
Gozzi, Carlo, 12

Graham, Martha, 92
Great Dictator, The, 215
Greene, Graham, 95
Guilbert, Yvette, 91

Hamlet, 8, 63, 73, 81, 148
Harbage, Alfred, 82
Harrison, Jane, 61, 63, 70–
 71, 72, 85
Hauptmann, Gerhart, 115,
 116
Hedda Gabler, 112
Hegel, Georg W. F., 200
Heine, Heinrich, 12
Hellman, Lillian, 12, 39, 40
Hemingway, Ernest, 6
Henry IV (of Pirandello) ,
 146
Henry V, 131
High Noon, 7
Hitler, Adolf, 126, 132, 133,
 198, 214, 215, 217, 219
Hochhuth, Rolf, 197, 198,
 201, 205–220, 224–227,
 228, 231
Hochwälder, Fritz, 30
Hofmannsthal, Hugo von,
 194
Homolka, Oscar, 104
Hoover, J. Edgar, 198
Hopwood, Avery, 88
Hotson, Leslie, 64
Houseman, John, 18
How Not to Write a Play, 78

Ibsen, Henrik, 5, 14, 41, 62,
 91, 98–118, 144, 173, 183–
 184

Index

Iceman Cometh, The, 34
Ionesco, Eugène, 157, 201
In the Summer House, 43
Inge, William, 28, 40, 42, 43
Inmost Leaf, The, 78
Ivanov, Vyacheslav, 75
Ivanov, 169, 170
Izenour, George, 29

James, William, 230
John xxiii, Pope, 217
John Gabriel Borkman, 112
Jones, Henry Arthur, 5

Kaiser, Georg, 130
Kanin, Garson, 32
Kazan, Elia, 30, 37
Kazin, Alfred, 78
Kerr, Clark, 230
Kerr, Jean, 33
Kerr, Walter, 20, 78–83, 87
Khan, Aly, 175
King, Martin Luther, 217
King Lear, 68–69, 145, 147, 160
King of Hearts, 33
Kingsley, Sidney, 34, 35, 40
Kismet, 18, 31
Kleist, Heinrich von, 150
Knott, Frederick, 7
Koestler, Arthur, 34, 35, 40
Kott, Jan, 203

Labiche, Eugène, 89
Lark, The, 52, 88
Lawrence, D. H., 63

League of Youth, The, 112
Lederer, Charles, 18, 31
Life with Father, 18
Life with Mother, 18
Lindsay, Howard, 18, 33
Lippmann, Walter, xiii, xiv, 217
Logan, Joshua, 42
Lonely Crowd, The, 49
Lopokova, Lydia, 101
Lord Jim, 75
Love's Labor's Lost, 66
Lowell, Robert, 159
Lower Depths, The, 40

Macbeth, 67, 182
Machiavelli, 164
Male Animal, The, 14, 31, 32
Man and Superman, 86, 129–130
Mann, Thomas, 171
Marat/Sade, 201
Marty, 80
Marx, Karl, 107, 200, 201
Massnahme, Die (The Measures Taken), 106, 115
Master Builder, The, 62, 101, 104
Maugham, Somerset, 74
Mauriac, François, 9, 51
McCarthy, Senator Joseph C., 11, 36, 39
McCarthy, Mary, 57
McCullers, Carson, 40, 41, 42
Mehring, Franz, 107
Member of the Wedding, The, 41, 42

Men of Distinction, 33
Meyerhold, V. E., 123, 184
*Midsummer Night's Dream,
A*, 65
Miller, Arthur, 11, 14, 24,
28, 30, 34, 35–40, 51, 84,
95, 114, 144, 145, 153, 182
Milton, John, 141
Misanthrope, The, 63
Miss Julie, 44
Molière, 12, 63, 97, 170, 171,
179, 184
Montherlant, Henri de, 9, 91
Morgenthau, Hans, xii, xiii,
xiv
Mother Courage, 95–96, 154,
155, 156
Mourning Becomes Electra,
75, 182
Mozart, Wolfgang A., 91, 97,
141, 199
Murder in the Cathedral,
134, 228
Mussolini, Benito, 90
*My Heart's in the High-
lands*, 18

Neher, Caspar, 28
Ney, Marie, 102
Nichols, Anne, 88, 165
Nicoll, Allardyce, 82
Niemöller, Martin, 134
Nietzsche, Friedrich, 92
1984, 21, 143
Nugent, Elliott, 14, 31, 32

Obey, André, 9

O'Casey, Sean, 4, 9
Odets, Clifford, 12, 34, 125
Oedipus Rex, 62, 160
Offenbach, Jacques, 89
O'Neill, Eugene, 14, 34, 74–
75, 76, 173, 182, 185
Oresteia, The, 63, 64, 183
Orpheus (of Cocteau), 185
Ortega y Gasset, José, 72, 92
Orwell, George, 21, 143
Osborne, John, 201
Otto, Teo, 28

Partage de Midi, Le, 9
Pasternak, Boris, 121, 194,
195
Peer Gynt, 111, 118
Pericles, 64
Phèdre, 160
Picnic, 28, 42, 43
Pirandello, Luigi, 55, 146,
174, 206
Pius XII, Pope, 197, 198, 207–
214, 218–220, 225
Plato, 64, 90, 119, 120, 123,
130
Playwright at Work, 40–44
Pompadour, Madame de, 91
Power of Darkness, The, 40
Prescott Papers, The, 33
Prince of Homburg, The,
150
Prisoner of Zenda, A, 7

Racine, Jean, 98, 151, 160
Radek, Karl, 106
Rajk, Làslò, 106

Index

Regan, Sylvia, 20, 21
Resurrection, 141
Richard III, 84
Riesman, David, 49, 111
Rinehart, Mary Roberts, 88
Rose Tattoo, The, 28
Rosmersholm, 103
Russell, Bertrand, 217

Saint Joan, 8, 211, 212, 220
Saint Joan of the Stockyards, 133
Salacrou, Armand, 9
Saroyan, William, 18
Sartre, Jean Paul, 9, 51, 196, 197, 200
Schiller, Friedrich, 73, 79, 98, 179, 212, 213, 214, 220
Schlesinger, Arthur M., Jr., 52
Schoenberg, Arnold, 199
Schweitzer, Albert, 137
Scribe, Eugène, 90, 101
Señora Carrar's Rifles, 129
Shakespeare, William, 5, 8, 9, 10, 14, 32, 63, 64–70, 73, 81, 82, 84, 85, 88, 90, 97, 117, 124, 128, 131, 144, 145, 147, 148, 152, 160, 165, 170, 171, 178, 179, 182
Shaw, George Bernard, 4, 9, 32, 46, 52, 62, 85, 86, 88, 91, 99, 129–130, 146, 173, 174, 179, 184, 211, 212, 213, 215, 220, 225
Shaw, Irwin, 26
Shelley, Percy B., 72

Sights and Spectacles, 57
Six Characters in Search of an Author, 55
Skulnik, Menasha, 20
Slansky, Rudolf, 106
Socrates, 130
Sophocles, 62, 160, 184, 220
Soulier de Satin, Le, 9
Spellman, Joseph Cardinal, 209
Stalin, Joseph, 11, 137
Stanislavsky, Constantin, 184
Stevens, Wallace, 194, 195
Storm Over the Deputy, The, 224
Stowe, Harriet Beecher, 120, 121
Stravinsky, Igor, 180
Streetcar Named Desire, A, 28, 30, 44
Strindberg, August, 44, 99, 113, 183
Strong Are Lonely, The, 30

Tea and Sympathy, 30
Tempest, The, 65–66, 68
Tetzel, Joan, 104
Theatrical World of 1897, The, 84
Thorndike, Sybil, 100
Threepenny Opera, The, 96, 221
Thurber, James, 12, 14, 31, 32
Titus Andronicus, 8
Tolstoy, Leo, 40, 119–120, 141, 146, 174, 178

Toynbee, Arnold, 217
*Treasure of Sierra Madre,
    The,* 7
Trilling, Lionel, 107, 144,
    145
Twelfth Night, 64
Two for the Seesaw, 144

Ulbricht, Walter, 203
Uncle Tom's Cabin, 120

Viereck, Peter, 90
View from the Bridge, A,
    182
Vilar, Jean, 149, 177
Voltaire, 91

Waiting for Godot, 157, 190,
    202–203, 204
Waiting for Lefty, 125
Walbrook, Anton, 103

Walser, Martin, 201
Warren, Robert Penn, 6
Waste Land, The, 134
Webster, Margaret, 30
Weill, Kurt, 199
Weiss, Peter, 201
What is Theatre?, 95
Wild Duck, The, 103, 108,
    109–110, 118
Wilde, Oscar, 32, 194–195,
    199
Williams, Emlyn, 102
Williams, Tennessee, 18, 24,
    28, 30, 40, 41, 44, 95
Willingham, Calder, 40
Winter's Tale, The, 66, 67
Wouk, Herman, 40, 51

Young, Stark, 26, 27

Zimmermann, Rolf, 224
Zola, Emile, 183